felted Crochet

Jane Davis

©2005 Jane Davis
Published by

kp books
An Imprint of F+W Publications

700 East State Street • Iola, WI 54990-0001
715-445-2214 • 888-457-2873

Our toll-free number to place an order or obtain a free catalog is
(800) 258-0929.

Library of Congress Catalog Number: 2005922940
ISBN: 0-87349-887-9

Edited by Maria L. Turner and Sarah Herman
Designed by Marilyn McGrane

Printed in the United States of America

acknowledgments

Thank you Maria Turner and Sarah Herman, my wonderful, talented editors, for all of your attention to details, your patience and understanding at deadlines, and your honest criticism and encouragement that always help these books come to fruition. It's been a pleasure to work with you.

Thank you to Corinne Loomer for your suggestion to write a book about felted crochet. It was something I had been pondering, but your voicing the idea made me see that it was definitely an area that needed a book.

Thank you to all the yarn companies whose fabulous yarns are the inspiration for project after project. They are:

- Baabajoes
- Berocco
- Brown Sheep
- Classic Elite Yarns
- Dale of Norway
- Lion Brand Yarns
- Harrisville Designs Yarns
- Ironstone Yarns
- Mountain Colors
- Noro
- Patons
- Tahki/Stacy Charles

Finally, thank you to my family, who have put up with yarn everywhere and frantic moments when deadlines loomed. You may never understand my excitement with yarn, but I thank you for living with it.

table of contents

introduction

Crocheting and felting are a wonderful combination of technique and texture, and the unique qualities of crochet make it especially suited for felting. Using basic crochet stitches and simple forms, you can create beautiful felted items from easy place mats to large blankets. Felted surfaces are wonderful backdrops for embroidery and beadwork, and can also be combined with nonfelted crocheting and novelty yarn to make rich, textural creations.

With crochet especially, there is the added benefit of possibilities in pattern design, since many crochet stitches retain more of their structure in the felting process than knitwear does when felted. Because the very nature of crochet is to create fabric from knots, the finished work is more firmly structured than knit work (which is more of a twisting of yarn). Therefore, when you felt crochetwork that has eyelets and holes, those holes don't disappear as much as they would if they were knitted. With crochet, you can felt filet mesh or decorative doilies, and instead of ending up with a faint shadow of the original design, you have the design still there—strong and beautiful, softened around the edges, or fuzzy and muted.

Crochet can also be very firm and structural when worked in tight single-crochet stitches, so it is easy to create freestanding creations like bowls and containers, which are more flimsy when worked in knitting.

In this book, you will find projects that explore these felted crochet advantages, as well as quick-and-easy items that are just fun to felt. You'll also find that many of the projects in this book work well as finished pieces without felting, so you have the option to felt or not to felt.

Crochet and felting are simple techniques at heart, with just a few things really happening. In crochet, you merely take a hook and some yarn, and then pull through loop after loop to create a fabric, while felting is just creating matted fibers. Isn't it amazing what can be achieved with these two simple processes?

chapter one

basics

Here is everything you need to know to get started with felting and crochet, from a basic crochet stitch primer to the step-by-step how-to of felting in the washing machine or by hand. Also covered are types of yarn to use in felting, how to prepare your work for felting and how to care for it after you've felted it. Plus, the basics of crochet, including stitches, abbreviations and tools used, are outlined for reference.

Crochet items, felted and nonfelted.

Swatches felted to varying degrees.

all about felting in crochet

felting

The process of felting is taking loose wool fibers and rubbing them until they mat together into a permanent fabric. The amazing transformation from loose fibers to felt results because each wool fiber is covered with tiny scales that relax, opening away from the fiber when they are warm and wet. When cooled, they pull tightly against the shaft of the fiber.

If you take a lot of these fibers and rub them against each other when the fibers are warm, wet and soapy, the scales open and get tangled together from one fiber to the other, so when they cool down and the scales try to close back to the shaft of the fiber, they all lock together into a fuzzy new arrangement that we call felt.

Felted fabric is technically not felted; it's *fulled*. Fulling occurs when you take a knitted, woven or crocheted fabric and felt it. But whatever the term, the process has the potential to create new textures in crochet.

degrees of feltedness

Because felting is a process, you have the option of stopping the felting at any point to achieve the finished look you want in your project. You can felt it just a little bit so there is still a great deal of stitch definition and just a little bit of fuzziness to the item. Or, you can felt it until it's so fuzzy you can't see the stitches at all, even when you hold the piece up to the light. Generally, you will felt a piece to get the desired shape and size you want for your finished project, but the amount of felting you want in your finished item really is a personal decision that can be different from piece to piece.

Felting can change the look of yarn patterns, like stripes.

Felting adds texture and can create a sense of realism, like with this flower.

unpredictable felt

Although there are specific, predictable processes that need to occur to cause wool fibers to felt, that doesn't mean that every time you make and felt the same project, it will come out exactly the same.

Home felting is not an exact science. It's a process of trial-and-error, and even with a large amount of experience in felting, you may still have times when you are surprised when a project doesn't felt the way you planned.

This is especially true with machine felting because when you close that washing machine lid, you don't get to see what goes on inside. Is the strap getting caught on a part of the agitator? Is the piece just staying in one place and only felting a little bit on one side? Is the project stretching out in an awkward shape and felting that way?

Due to the unknowns in machine-felting, it's important to check your project often, especially if it's a large project or an item like a hat that would be ruined if it shrunk too much or became so misshapen that it couldn't be pulled back into form.

In hand-felting, you have more control, but there is still the question of the type of yarn used from project to project, how the wool is rubbed, the type of soap used and how hard

the water is. The wool itself can be a little different from season to season, depending on what the sheep ate while the wool grew and even the weather conditions at the time.

Your yarn not only changes texture in the felting process, it can also end up with subtle color changes, depending on the yarn used and if you have mixed different colors or types of yarn in the same piece. Different colored stripes, for example, soften along the edges, while darker colors may tint lighter. A single-colored yarn may not be completely colorfast and may fade slightly from the hot water. Tweedy, textured yarn sometimes blends into an all-over color that is less distinct. And variegated yarns soften and blend like the stripes. These changes can be happy transformations or surprising losses in your expectations of the finished project, so it is always a good idea to felt a sample when you plan to use variegated yarn or mix colors such as in stripes. A test sample will enable you to have a good idea of how your yarn will handle.

So with felting, you can never really be completely sure what you will get in the end, but that's part of the fun and discovery of this technique that makes it so interesting.

A variety of feltable yarns.

Swatches and a small project.

yarns to felt

Feltable yarn isn't just made from sheep's wool. You can also felt yarn that is made from alpaca, mohair and blends of yarn, to name a few options. Just about any yarn that is at least 50 percent animal fiber and hasn't been treated to protect against felting can be felted. Any yarn labels that read "machine washable" have been treated so they won't felt, so stay away from those for your felting projects.

You will find that some yarns felt more quickly and easily than others. Alpaca tends to take a little longer to felt, but has a beautiful finished texture once it is fully felted. Any yarn that has mohair in its make-up will have a furrier surface than one that is just sheep's wool, so you have choices for texture even in your finished felt!

novelty yarns

Novelty yarns, such as the long-stranded furry eyelash yarns, are usually made of all, or mostly, synthetic fibers that do not felt. There are some novelty yarns that blend wool, mohair and/or alpaca with synthetic fibers, and if these are not treated to be machine-washable, they will felt to some degree. Adding these non-felting or semifelting yarns to your crochet can achieve some wonderful effects. The Fuzzy Striped Blanket, page 84, combines the warmth of the felted wool with the soft silkiness of the eyelash yarn to make a blanket that has the best of both worlds of yarn qualities.

making a swatch

Making and felting a swatch of your yarn in the intended stitch for the project is an important part of the process. It will tell you a lot about how the yarn behaves when felted, from any color changes to the finished texture to the general shrinkage amount. What it won't tell you is how a larger or oddly-shaped piece will felt, or how a piece will felt in the washer if you are felting your swatch by hand. But it is good to have a beginning gauge, since many yarns change a lot from swatch to felted swatch. I like to use smaller projects such as small bags or coasters for my test swatches. That way, I have made a project as well as tested out my yarn.

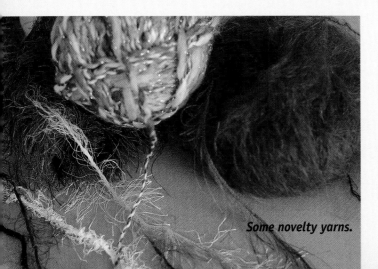

Some novelty yarns.

Three swatches worked in different size hooks and felted.

Projects with basted openings, ready to felt.

tension for felting

Many felting patterns instruct you to make your project with very loose stitches. They also suggest you make the prefelted piece much larger than your finished piece. While it is exciting to see the transformation from a loose, limp shape to a dense, firm finished piece, that method is not the only successful way to felt.

Your project will still felt successfully, even if you work in a tight tension. It just won't shrink quite as much. Generally, crochet shrinks about 25 percent to 30 percent vertically and 10 percent to 20 percent horizontally in the felting process. This is, of course, dependent on how much time you felt your project, but it is a good guideline when planning.

For items like the stuffed animals and Pumpkin Pincushion on page 102, you need to keep your tension from being too loose, as the stuffing will poke through in the felting process and distort the finished piece.

preparing to felt

Any openings tend to flare out at the edges when the item is felted in the washing machine. Unless you want such openings to flare out more than they are before felting, you will want to consider several options for adjusting the flare.

One option is to make the opening smaller than you want the opening in the finished item to be, such as in the Stiff Yarn Bowl on page 74 or the Circular Rug on page 86.

Another remedy is to baste the edges

Felting by machine.

TIP: For step 5 below, I usually place wet felted pieces either in my oven or on top of the dryer. When I put a piece in the oven, I first set the oven between 200 and 250 degrees to warm it up, turn off the heat and then set the item on a cookie sheet covered with a dish towel. I let the piece dry inside overnight. Large items get hung outside in the shade or are sometimes put in the dryer if they can take a little more felting, which will shrink them a bit more.

all about felting in crochet

felting by washing machine

Felting by machine is my method of choice for most projects, unless they are very small and wouldn't felt well in the machine.

Start by setting the washer to the hot-wash/cold-rinse setting on the lowest water level your washer allows, put some liquid dish soap (I use Ivory dish soap) and add in a non-pilling cotton fabric item with the crochetwork to help add friction.

It seems that everyone who felts has her own particular method of felting and the following is the way I felt projects in the washing machine. You will need to experiment to see what works for you.

1. Put about 1 tablespoon of Ivory dish soap in the machine and set the wash to hot-wash/cold-rinse and the water level to the lowest level.

2. Add in a natural off-white canvas bag (or other non-pilling cotton fabric item) and the crochetwork to be felted.

3. Set the washer to the normal cycle setting for an eight-minute wash.

4. Check the item part way through, just after the wash cycle when the water has been drained out, in the middle of the rinse cycle, and again just after the rinse cycle. If at any of these times, the item is felted as much as desired, do one of two things.

- If the item and the machine are not soapy (when it's past the wash cycle or part way through the rinse cycle), set the machine to the spin cycle to get most of the water out of the project.
- If the item and machine are soapy (when it's still in the wash cycle or in the beginning of the rinse cycle), take the item out of the machine and rinse it in cold water by hand. Set the machine to the rinse cycle so all the soap gets washed out, put the crochetwork back in the machine and set it to the spin cycle so that it gets as much water out of the crochetwork as possible.

5. Take the item and pull, push or nudge it into the finished shape desired and put it in a warm, dry place to dry.

TIP: If you've felted before, you may notice that I don't mention putting your crochetwork into a mesh bag before you put it in the washing machine. Many instructions say to do this so that you won't clog up your machine with the massive amount of loose wool that fuzzes off the project as it is felted. I worried about this when I first began felting, but found that there was too much restriction of the project in the mesh bag and that it never seemed to felt as evenly as when it was able to agitate freely in the machine. I also was frustrated when having to remove the wet item from the wet bag to see how it was doing. So, with much anxiety about a possible call to the repairman if my machine got clogged, I began felting all my projects without putting them in the mesh bag. So far, I have had no problems, but I encourage you to try the bag first to see if you are comfortable with it so you don't have to worry about damaging your machine.

Details to Note

What kind of soap to use: Use a pure soap, like Ivory dish soap. The addition of soap helps soften the fibers so they tangle together more, which aids in the felting process. Since Ivory brand is the one that I have always used, I can't say if there is a difference with other non-pure soap brands. If you find that your item isn't felting well though, try a different liquid soap.

What kind of cotton fabric to add: Don't ever put a terry cloth towel, or other item that sheds, in with your felting unless you want little bits of it permanently stuck to your project piece. Thick cotton, such as an undyed denim or twill, is a great addition to help your item felt faster because it aids with the agitation. Make sure there are no raw edges that can fray. I would not put anything that has a color that might come off in the washer unless you aren't concerned if the color gets into your felting. So, blue jeans are OK for blue projects, but not for white ones.

How to monitor the process: Checking on the item at various stages of the wash cycle is more important for some items than for others. Anything that needs to fit something else, like a hat or slipper, needs to be checked often because you want to make sure it doesn't felt smaller than you want it. Checking often on things like bags and stuffed animals is less critical. If I am sure it won't matter how small an item gets, I will just let the washer run its course and check it at the end of the complete cycle.

Felting by hand.

TIP: For step 2 below, I sometimes add ice cubes to the cold water to get it very cold, though getting the water cold this way is optional.

all about felting in crochet

felting by hand

Felting by hand can be very rewarding because you get to witness the amazing transformation from crocheted yarn to felt. It is impractical for large items because of the amount of rubbing it takes, but it is ideal for small items. Here is the method I use to felt by hand.

1. Put about 1 teaspoon of liquid dish soap (I use Ivory brand) in a large bowl, add hot tap water and place the crochetwork in the bowl to soak.

2. Get a bowl of cold water ready and set it next to the first bowl.

3. Hold the crochetwork in the soapy water, rub it between your hands, rub it on itself and change direction of rubbing. Keep rubbing the piece until it starts to mat together, which can take several minutes.

4. Dip the piece in the cold water and keep rubbing, watching to see if it is felted as desired. If it isn't felted enough, let it soak back in the hot soapy water and repeat the whole process as much as you need to achieve your desired feltedness.

5. Rinse the item in cool tap water and press out as much water as you can.

6. Roll the piece up tightly in a clean, dry towel to remove as much water as possible.

7. Use your hands to shape as needed.

8. Dry in a warm, dry place, as suggested in the step 5 tip for felting by washing machine, page 14.

Unblocked and blocked projects.

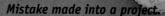

Mistake made into a project.

blocking

When your piece is felted, you still may need to adjust it before it dries to get it into its final shape. This adjustment can include anything from putting a hat on your head for a few minutes so it shapes to your head to pulling a filet-netted piece into shape and pinning it to dry, just as you would with a fine lace doily. Bags usually need to be shaped into their desired finished shape before drying. Anything you can do to form your piece the way you want it is OK, from wadding up plastic or paper covered in plastic to shape a bag to stretching and pulling a piece into shape.

fixing mistakes

No matter how many times you try felting, there will always be those instances when your project just doesn't come out the way you expect. Use such opportunities to explore your creative side a little further. Try cutting the piece and sewing it together into something else. Or cut the mistake into circles, squares, hearts or flowers and use them for coasters or to make small bags. If you can't make something beautiful from your goof, you can still use it for something utilitarian. Felt makes a good dry marker eraser for white boards and it's a good duster or hotpad.

Finished felted projects.

caring for felted items

Once your project is felted, it can never go back to what it was, but it can keep shrinking if you wash it or put it in the dryer again. So, when you have your finished piece the way you want it, treat it like any of your other fine nonwashable crochetwork and hand wash it, or wash it on a delicate cycle with cool water and hand washable soaps. Squeeze excess water out of it with a clean towel and let it dry in a warm, dry place. If your piece has dyed colors, keep it out of direct sunlight, just in case it isn't fade-proof.

Crochet swatches in various yarn and hook sizes.

crochet terms and abbreviations

standard yarn weight system and skill levels

standard yarn weight system

Recently, yarn industry designers, manufacturers and publishers adopted a standardized system to help crocheters understand the various yarn weights and hook sizes. These symbols, which appear on the yarn labels, are incorporated into each project in this book to make it easier for you to choose your own yarn variations. Use the chart as a guideline, as it reflects the most commonly used gauges and hook sizes for specific yarn categories.

Yarn Weight Symbol and Category Names	SUPER FINE 1 SUPER FIN Super Fino	FINE 2 FIN Fino	LIGHT 3 LEGER Ligero	MEDIUM 4 MOYEN Medio	BULKY 5 BULKY Abultado	SUPER BULKY 6 SUPER BULKY Super Abultado
Types of Yarns in a Category	Sock, Fingering, Baby	Sport, Baby	DK, Light, Worsted	Worsted, Afghan, Aran	Chunky, Craft, Rug	Bulky, Roving
Crochet Gauge Range in Single Crochet (sc) to 4"	21 to 32 sts	16 to 20 sts	12 to 17 sts	11 to 14 sts	8 to 11 sts	5 to 9 sts
Recommended Metric Hook Size Range	2.25mm to 3.5mm	3.5mm to 4.5mm	4.5mm to 5.5mm	5.5mm to 6.5mm	6.5mm to 9mm	9mm and larger
Recommended U.S. Hook Size Range	#B-1 to #E-4	#E-4 to #7	#7 to #I-9	#I-9 to #K-10½	#K-10½ to #M-13	#M-13 and larger

skill levels

A set of standard skill level icons also was introduced recently to the industry by the Craft Yarn Council of America. Each project in this book contains a skill level icon to guide you.

BEGINNER	Projects for first-time crocheters, using basic stitches and minimal shaping.
EASY	Projects using yarn with basic stitches, repetitive stitch patterns, simple color changes, and simple shaping and finishing.
INTERMEDIATE	Projects using a variety of techniques, such as basic lace patterns or color patterns, mid-level shaping and finishing.
EXPERIENCED	Projects with intricate stitch patterns, techniques and dimension, such as non-repeating patterns, multicolor techniques, fine threads, small hooks, detailed shaping and refined finishing.

crochet terms and abbreviations

the yarn label

The label around your yarn contains several useful tidbits. Read the label carefully, as it divulges: yarn content; length of yarn in yards and meters; weight in ounces and grams; suggested crochet hook size and the resulting gauge; dye lot number; color name and number; and care instructions.

The care instructions are shown as symbols, as identified in the accompanying chart.

Additional symbols appear on labels to designate the various weights or thicknesses of yarns. A number from one to six is assigned, with one the finest weight and six the thickest (see the Standard Yarn Weight Systems information on page 18).

Washing

⊠	Do not wash
〰	Hand-wash in warm water
30°	Hand-wash at temperature stated
⊡	Machine wash
⊠	Do not tumble dry
◯	Tumble drying acceptable
⊟	Dry flat
⊠	No bleach
△CL	Chlorine bleach acceptable

Pressing

⊠	Do not iron
⊡	Cool iron
⊡⊡	Warm iron
⊡⊡⊡	Hot iron

Dry Cleaning

⊗	Do not dry clean
Ⓐ	Dry cleanable in all solvents
Ⓕ	Dry cleanable with fluorocarbon or petroleum-based solvents only
Ⓟ	Dry cleanable with perchlorethylene, hydrocarbons, or petroleum-based solvent

gauge

Just as with nonfelted projects, you will need to check your gauge before beginning your project. However, for many of the projects in this book, gauge is not as critical as in non-felting books, since the item is going to shrink in the felting process anyway. For items such as the toys in Chapter 6, you need to have a fairly tight tension so that the stuffing doesn't distort the project when felting.

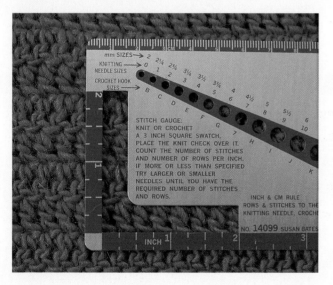

American vs. European crochet stitch terms conversion

Here is a common conversion chart for U.S. and European stitch terms. All the projects in this book are written using U.S. terms.

U.S.	European
Single crochet (sc)	Double crochet
Slip stitch (sl st)	Single crochet
Half double crochet (hdc)	Half treble crochet
Double crochet (dc)	Treble crochet
Triple crochet (tr)	Double treble

crochet terms and abbreviations

crochet abbreviations

If you are a beginner looking at crochet instructions for the first time, the abbreviations may seem a bit overwhelming. The following list is meant to help identify some of the more commonly used abbreviations in this book. In time and with practice, such crocheting shorthand becomes second nature.

Abbreviation	Description
approx	approximately
beg	begin, beginning
ch	chain
ch-	refers to chain or space previously made: e.g., ch-1 space
ch-sp	chain space
CL	cluster
cm	centimeter(s)
cont	continue
dc	double crochet
dec	decrease/decreases/decreasing
ea	each
foll	follow/follows/following
g	gram(s)
hdc	half double crochet
hk	hook
inc	increase/increases/increasing
lp(s)	loop(s)

Abbreviation	Description
m	meter(s)
mm	millimeter(s)
oz	ounce(s)
patt	pattern
pm	place marker
prev	previous
rem	remaining
rep	repeat
rnd(s)	round(s)
sc	single crochet
sk	skip
Sl st	slip sitich
sp(s)	space(s)
st(s)	stitch(es)
tog	together
tr	treble crochet
yo	yarn over

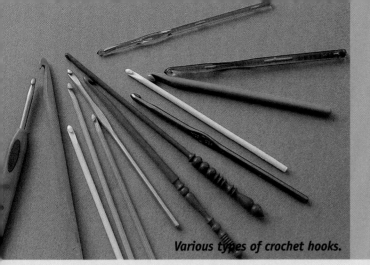

Various types of crochet hooks.

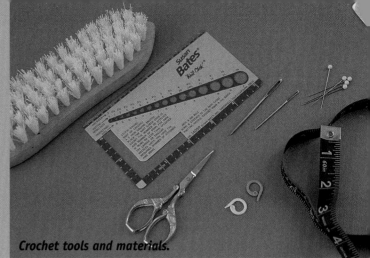

Crochet tools and materials.

crochet hooks

Crochet hooks come in a variety of sizes, types and materials, including aluminum, plastic, wood and bamboo.

Basic hooks: These are usually 6" to 7" long with a hook at one end. They can be sold in sets with a variety of sizes, or individually. Standard U.S. sizes range from B to K with some additional larger sizes for bulkier yarns and smaller steel hooks for thread crochet. Many hooks have both the U.S. sizes and the diameter in millimeters.

Afghan hooks: These are used to crochet in afghan stitch, which is a technique in which you pick up stitches across a row in one direction, then work the stitches off the hook on the next row in the opposite direction. Afghan hooks can be long with a hook at one end and a stop at the far end like a knitting needle, or they can have a flexible shaft.

Double-pointed hooks: These are used for a new technique called crochetknit, or if they have a different sized hook at each end, they are just an option for standard crochet with two hook sizes in one.

other crocheting tools

While the yarn and crochet hooks are the most basic of tools needed, you may also want to consider adding the following list of specialty items to your yarn basket.

Brush: Used to soften finished felted projects.

Large-head pins: Used to pin crocheted pieces together for sewing and to block finished pieces on a flat surface.

Stitch gauge: Used to measure crocheted gauge.

Stitch markers (open ended): Used to mark increases, decreases and pattern changes.

Yarn needle or **large-sized tapestry needle:** Used to seam finished pieces together or weave in yarn ends.

In addition to the special crocheting tools, a good pair of sharp **scissors**, a **measuring tape** and an **iron** should also be on hand.

Crochet Hook Conversion

Here is a common conversion chart for U.S. and metric hook sizes, though you will occasionally find some variances in conversions.

U.S.	Metric (mm)	U.S.	Metric (mm)	U.S.	Metric (mm)
B-1	2.25	G-7	4.5	M/N-13	9
C-2	2.75	H-8	5	N/P-15	10
D-3	3.25	I-9	5.5	P/Q	15
E-4	3.5	J-10	6	Q	16
F-5	3.75	K-10½	6.5	S	19
G-6	4	L-11	8		

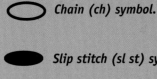 *Chain (ch) symbol.*

Slip stitch (sl st) symbol.

 Single crochet (sc) symbol.

basic crocheting techniques

slip knot

1. Make a loop.

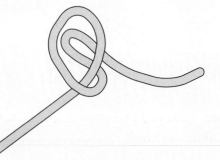

2. Push the working end of the yarn up through the back of the loop.

3. Slide the hook through the loop and tighten by pulling on both ends of the yarn.

chain

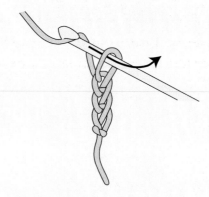

1. Begin with a slip knot. Yarn over.

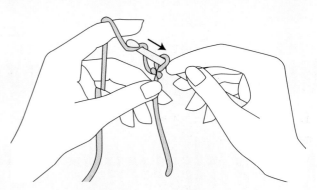

2. Pull through loop on hook.

slip stitch

single crochet

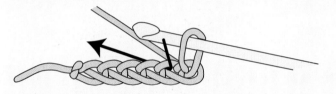

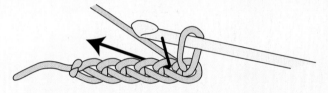

1. Insert the hook from front to back into the next stitch or chain.

1. Insert the hook from front to back into the next stitch or chain.

2. Yarn over, pull through stitch or chain and the loop on the hook (one loop on hook).

2. Yarn over, pull through stitch or chain (two loops on hook).

3. Yarn over, pull through both loops on hook (one loop on hook).

Half double crochet (hdc) symbol. *Double crochet (dc) symbol.* *Triple crochet (tc) symbol.*

basic crocheting techniques

half double crochet

1. Yarn over, insert the hook from front to back into the next stitch or third chain from hook.

2. Yarn over, pull through stitch or chain (three loops on hook).

3. Yarn over, pull through all three loops on hook (one loop on hook).

double crochet

1. Yarn over, insert the hook from front to back into the next stitch or fourth chain from hook.

2. Yarn over, pull through stitch or chain (three loops on hook).

3. Yarn over, pull through two loops on hook (two loops on hook).

4. Yarn over, pull through remaining two loops on hook (one loop on hook).

triple crochet

1. Yarn over twice, insert the hook from front to back into the next stitch or fifth chain from hook.

2. Yarn over, pull through stitch or chain (four loops on hook).

3. Yarn over, pull through two loops on hook (three loops on hook).

4. Yarn over, pull through two loops on hook (two loops on hook).

5. Yarn over, pull through remaining two loops on hook (one loop on hook).

weaving in tail

In most cases, to weave in loose ends of yarn in crocheting, you don't want to make knots and you don't want the yarn to show on the right side of the fabric. Thread the tail with a blunt ended tapestry needle and pass through the crochetwork, hiding the yarn for about 1" to 2". Cut the remaining tail close to the crochet surface.

chapter two

bags and purses

Bags and purses are by far some of the easiest and most fun projects to felt. You don't have to worry about fit, so it doesn't matter if the bag shrinks too much, and you can practice with all sorts of experiments from colorwork and embroidery to lace and ruffles. Since they are relatively small, you are not investing a great deal of time and money, and since you don't have to "wear" them, if they don't come out the way you like, you can still use them at home to hold an in-progress project or to store yarn. Here are just a few ideas ranging from a simple drawstring bag to a more detailed bag with embroidery, a doily-type flap and tassel.

This is a really easy project that is a great introduction to felting. Just make a circle, and then work even, without increases, until it's a little taller than you want it. Then, cinch the top of the bag closed before felting, ensuring success no matter how long you agitate your project in the washer. This is a great project to experiment with different combinations of yarn, such as the tweedy dark wool and sparkly lime yarns that were used in the sample project. You may be surprised at how different yarns look before and after felting.

small project bag

EASY

4 MEDIUM 2 FINE

Finished Size Before Felting
5" diameter at base x 8" tall

Finished Size After Felting
5" diameter at base x 7" tall

Stitches Used
ch
sc
hdc
dc

Gauge in Single Crochet
12 sts and 11 rows = 4"

Project before felting.

Project after felting.

materials

- 1 ball (183yd/167m) worsted weight wool yarn*
- 1 ball (198yd/180m) fine weight blend yarn*
- Size J (6 mm) hook
- Size D (3.25 mm) hook
- Stitch marker

*Used in this project: 1 skein Tahki's Donegeal Tweed (100% pure new wool, 183yd/167m, 3.5oz/ 100g), color #894, and 1 ball S. Charles Collezione's Ritratto (28% mohair/53% rayon/10% nylon/9% polyester, 198yd/180m, 1.75oz/ 50g), color #72.

instructions
bag

Use 1 strand of ea yarn held tog as 1 throughout and the larger hk.

Foundation: Ch 2, turn.

Rnd 1: 6 sc in 2nd ch from hk, pm, do not turn.

Rnd 2: 2 sc in ea st - 12 sts.

Rnd 3: (Sc in next st, 2 sc in next st) rep 6 times - 18 sts.

Rnd 4: (Sc in next 2 sts, 2 sc in next st) rep 6 times - 24 sts.

Cont with 6 inc in ea rnd until you work a rep of (sc in the next 7 sts, and 2 sc in the next st) for a total of 54 sts.

Work even in dc for 13 rnds.

To level off last rnd at rim, work hdc in next 3 sts, then sc in next 3 sts.

Weave in ends.

tie

Use the thin blend yarn and the smaller hk.

Foundation: Ch 150, turn.

Row 1: Ch 1, sc in 2nd ch from hk and ea ch across.

Weave in ends.

assembly

Thread one end of the tie with a large tapestry needle. Weave in and out of the second row from the top edge, passing over and under 5 stitches. For the last few stitches, you will need to pass over 3 or 4 stitches so that both ends meet on the outside of the bag. Tie the ends into a bow.

Weave the tie in and out along the second row of the top edge.

felting

Felt in the washer, checking occasionally to see if the bag is completely felted. When the bag is felted to the desired texture, adjust to the finished shape and let dry in a warm, dry place.

This quick little round purse is great to store your notions in, from stitch markers to tapestry needles to small scissors. It demonstrates an advantage of felted purses, since such small notions won't poke through the purse because the stitches are felted into a tight, firm surface. With the bead edging, you will always be able to fish it out of your project bag or basket by feel, and by choosing a beautiful multicolored yarn, it is nice to have it displayed on a table while you work.

bead-edged round coin purse

INTERMEDIATE

4 MEDIUM

Finished Size Before Felting
5¾" diameter

Finished Size After Felting
4¾" diameter

Stitches Used
ch
sc

Gauge in Single Crochet
16 sts and 18 rows = 4"

Project before felting.

Project after felting.

materials

- 1 ball (233yd/209m) worsted weight variegated wool yarn*
- Size I (5.5 mm) hook
- Stitch marker
- 7" zipper
- Cotton cord
- Tapestry needle
- Needle and thread to match yarn
- Size 11 beading needle
- Size B beading thread to match yarn
- Beads
  - 31 ¼" drop beads**
  - 190 size 11 seed beads**
  - 63 size 8 seed beads**
  - ¾"-long accent bead
  - ¼"-long faceted bead
  - 2 ⅛"-long faceted beads
  - 2 ¼"-wide disc beads

*Used in this project: 1 skein Lion Brand Yarn's Monet (100% virgin wool, 230yd/207m, 4oz/112g), color #404 Tropical Storm.

**Bead amounts are approximate and may vary slightly in your own beadwork.

instructions

(Make two.)

Foundation: Ch 2, turn.

Rnd 1: 6 sc in 2nd ch from hk, pm, do not turn.

Rnd 2: 2 sc in ea st - 12 sts.

Rnd 3: (Sc in next st, 2 sc in next st) rep 6 times - 18 sts.

Rnd 4: (Sc in next 2 sts, 2 sc in next st) rep 6 times - 24 sts.

Cont with 6 inc in ea rnd until you work a rep of (sc in the next 10 sts, and 2 sc in the next st) for a total of 72 sts.

Weave in ends.

felting

Baste both pieces together along the outer edges with cotton cord. Felt in the washer, checking occasionally until the purse is completely felted. Remove the basting stitches, adjust to the finished shape, and let dry in a warm, dry place.

assembly

Cut the zipper to 4" or 4½" long and take about 10 stitches around the cut end to hold it in place. Sew the zipper in place to each side of the bag with the needle and thread. Sew the rest of the edges of the bag together with the needle and thread.

beading

Using the beading thread and beading needle, follow the illustration below to sew the bead pattern to the edge of the bag. Make the beaded zipper pull and beaded loop as shown in the illustration at right.

- size 11 seed bead
- size 8 seed bead
- drop bead

Stitch beads along the sides as shown.

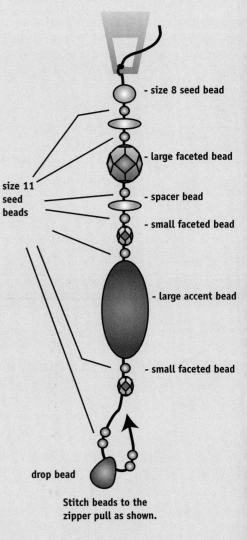

- size 8 seed bead
- large faceted bead
- spacer bead
- small faceted bead
- large accent bead
- small faceted bead

size 11 seed beads

drop bead

Stitch beads to the zipper pull as shown.

This project is only partially felted so you can clearly see the stitches. The case is quick and easy to make, being just a simple, straight bag. Then, after felting, you can turn down the front edge and embellish it with beads. The optional strap with the clasp lets you attach it to your bedpost or purse strap so you can quickly find your glasses in your purse or in the dark.

beaded eyeglasses case

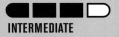

INTERMEDIATE

2 FINE

Finished Size Before Felting
  4" x 7"

Finished Size After Felting
  3¾" x 6"

Stitches Used
  ch
  hdc

Gauge in Half Double Crochet
  14 sts and 12 rows = 4"

Project after felting.

materials

- 1 ball (126yd/115m) fine weight wool yarn*
- Size F (3.75 mm) hook
- Stitch marker
- Cotton cord
- Tapestry needle
- Size 11 beading needle
- Size B beading thread to match yarn color
- Beads
    - 210 size 8 seed beads**
    - 60 size 8 cube beads**
    - 225 size 11 seed beads**
    - 15 ¼"-wide disc beads**
    - ¼"-long faceted bead
- Optional: clasp

*Used in this project: 1 ball Dale of Norway's Tiur (100% pure new wool, 126yd/115m, 1.75oz/50g), color #6222.
**Bead amounts are approximate and may vary slightly in your own beadwork.

instructions

Foundation: Ch 10, turn.

Rnd 1: Ch 2, working in the back half of the chs, hdc in 3rd ch from hk and ea ch across to last ch, 3 hdc in last ch, working in the other half of the chs, hdc in 8 ch, 3 hdc in last ch, pm, do not turn.

Rnd 2 - 18: Hdc in ea st around.

Weave in ends.

felting

Baste the opening closed with the cotton cord. Felt in the washer, checking occasionally to see if the case is completely felted. When the case is felted to the desired texture, remove the basting stitches, adjust to the finished shape and let dry in a warm, dry place.

beading

Using the beading thread and beading needle, follow the illustrations below to create the beaded strap, securing it on one end with stitches into the top corner of the bag and on the other end either with the optional clasp or with additional stitches directly into the bag.

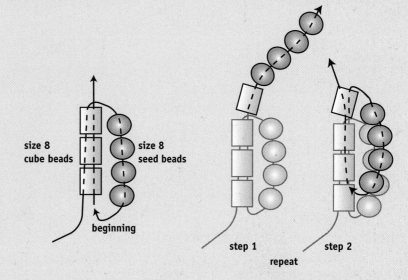

size 8 cube beads

size 8 seed beads

beginning

step 1

repeat

step 2

beaded eyeglasses case

Using the beading thread and beading needle, create the beaded embellishment on the upper edges of the bag by following the illustrations below.

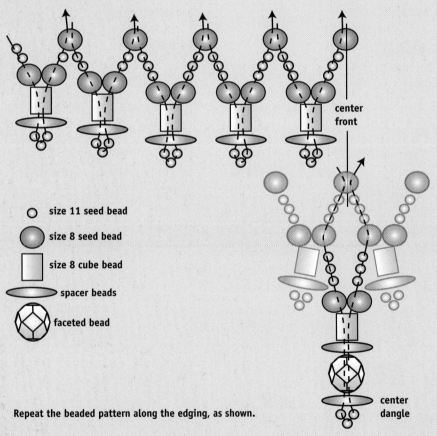

○ size 11 seed bead

● size 8 seed bead

▢ size 8 cube bead

⬭ spacer beads

⬡ faceted bead

center front

center dangle

Repeat the beaded pattern along the edging, as shown.

This easy-to-make bag is great for portable projects. The rich color transitioning yarn is beautifully shown off in the long, narrow shape and felts up to a nice fuzzy texture. Leave the opening as is or add a favorite button for a special closure.

quiver bag

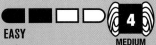

EASY

4 MEDIUM

Finished Size Before Felting
6" x 18" with 19"-long strap

Finished Size After Felting
5½" x 17" with a 27"-long
strap

Stitches Used
ch
sc
dc
sl st

Gauge in Double Crochet
15 sts and 8 rows = 4"

materials

- 2 skeins (110yd/101m)
worsted weight wool*
- Size H (5 mm) hook
- Cotton cord
- Tapestry needle
- Stitch marker

*Used in this project: 2 balls Noro's
Kureyon (100% wool, 110yd/101m,
1.75oz/50g), color #88.

Project before felting.

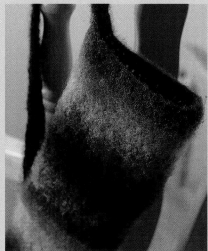
Project after felting.

instructions
bag

Foundation: Ch 4, turn.

Rnd 1: 10 dc in 4th ch from hk,
join into a circle with sl st in top
of ch-4, pm.

Rnd 2: 2 sc in ea st around and in
sl st - 22 sts.

Rnd 3: (2 sc in the next st, sc in
the next st) rep around - 33 sts.

Rnd 4: (2 sc in the next st, sc in
the next 2 sts) rep around - 44
sts.

Rnd 5 and 6: Sc in ea st around.

Row 7: Ch 2, dc in ea st around, sl
st in top of ch-2.

Row 8 - 35: Ch 3, dc in ea st
around, sl st in top of ch-3.

Do not weave in ends.

strap

Cont with the working yarn, sl st in
the next 3 sts, turn.

(Ch 3, dc in the next 6 sts, turn),
rep 38 times, or until just enough
yarn to sew end to bag.

Sew end to the 18th row from the
top opening of the bag.

Weave in ends.

felting

Baste the top opening closed with
cotton cord. Felt in the washer,
checking occasionally to see if the
bag is completely felted. When
the bag is felted to the desired
texture, remove the cotton cord,
adjust to the finished shape and
let dry in a warm, dry place.

Making this bag large or small and solid or striped is a cinch since it's just a flat circle folded in half. I made the sample project without a zipper, but you could also use a separating zipper along the whole edge so your bag opens flat for a working surface. If you made it really large, you could even make it into a portable baby rug.

half-moon bag

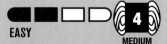
Finished Size Before Felting

22" x 10½" with 19"-long straps

Finished Size After Felting

19" x 8" with 22"-long straps

Stitches Used

ch

hdc

dc

sl st

Gauge in Double Crochet

14 sts and 7½ rows = 4"

Note

When counting sts in ea row on body of bag, ch-2 and ch-3 count as a st.

materials

- 7 balls (190yd/173m) worsted weight wool yarn*:
  - 2 blue
  - 1 pink
  - 1 turquoise
  - 1 white
  - 1 purple
  - 1 black
- Size I (5.5 mm) hook
- Cotton cord
- Tapestry needle
- Stitch marker

*Used in this project: Brown Sheep's Lamb's Pride (85% wool/15% mohair, 190yd/173m, 4 oz/113g), 2 skeins of color #M79 Blue Boy, and 1 skein each of colors #M-75 Blue Heirloom, #M-102 Orchid, #M62 Amethyst, #M05 Onyx and #M140 Aran.

Project before felting.

Project after felting.

instructions
bag

Foundation: Using the blue yarn ch 4, turn.

Rnd 1: 11 dc in 4th ch from hk, sl st in top of ch-4, pm, do not turn.

Rnd 2: Ch 3, 2 dc in ea st, dc in base of ch-3 - 24 sts.

Rnd 3: Change to pink yarn, ch 3, (2 dc in next st, dc in next st) rep 11 times, 2 dc in last st, sl st in top of ch-3 - 36 sts.

Rnd 4: Change to turquoise yarn, ch 3, (dc in next 2 sts, 2 dc in next st) rep 11 times, dc in next 2 sts, sl st in top of ch-3 - 48 sts.

Rnd 5: Ch 3, (dc in next 3 sts, 2 dc in next st) rep 11 times, dc in next 3 sts, sl st in top of ch-3 - 60 sts.

Rnd 6: Ch 3, (dc in next 4 sts, 2 dc in next st) rep 11 times, dc in next 4 sts, sl st in top of ch-3 - 72 sts.

Cont inc 12 sts ea rnd, working the following color sequence:
1 row white, 1 row purple, 2 rows blue, 1 row black, 1 row blue, 1 row turquoise, 1 row white, 1 row blue, 1 row pink, 2 rows blue, 1 row black, 2 rows turquoise

Fold the circle in half and sc through both halves for 30 sts.

Weave in ends.

Attach a new length of turquoise yarn through both layers of the circle, 30 sts from the other side of the fold and sc to the fold.

Weave in ends.

straps

(Make two.)

Foundation: Using the turquoise yarn, ch 4, turn.

Row 1: Ch 2, hdc in 3rd ch from hk and next 3 ch, turn - 4 sts.

Row 2: Ch 2, hdc in ea st across, turn.

Row 3: Ch 2, hdc in ea st across, do not turn.

To begin cord: Yo, insert hk in far left st from back to front, complete hdc.

Yo, insert hk in next st to right, from back to front, complete hdc.

Cont hdc in ea st working into the st from the back to the front and spiraling around to the right, until the cord is approx 18" from the beg.

To begin the flat section: Turn, ch 2, and work 4 hdc in the next 4 sts, turn. Work 2 more rows of hdc, cut yarn to about 6" and pull through last lp.

Use tails of yarn to sew handles to bag on the second-to-the-last rnd of the bag, centered over the inc sections on either side of the center front and back of the bag.

felting

Baste the opening of the bag closed with cotton cord. Felt in the washer, checking occasionally to see if the bag is completely felted. When the bag is felted to the desired texture, remove the basting cord, adjust to the finished shape, and let dry in a warm, dry place.

This elegant little bag is made special by all the finishing details, from the gimp covering the zipper's edge on the inside to the choice of beads for the zipper pull. Make it in red as shown, or use a favorite hand-dyed wool to make a unique and beautiful design. Even line it with silk to really finish it off!

red zipper purse

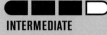

INTERMEDIATE

2 FINE

Finished Size Before Felting
4¾" x 7"

Finished Size After Felting
4½" x 7"

Stitches Used
ch
sc

Gauge in Single Crochet
16 sts and 22 rows = 4"

Project after felting.

materials

- 1 ball (126yd/115m) fine weight wool yarn*
- Size F (3.75 mm) hook
- Cotton cord
- Tapestry needle
- Stitch marker
- ¾ yard ³⁄₁₆"-wide gimp
- 7" zipper
- Sewing needle and thread to match yarn
- Size 11 beading needle
- Thread to match beads
- Beads
  - 10 size 11 seed beads**
  - 3 size 9 faceted metal beads
  - 2 ¼"-wide spacer beads
  - ¼"-wide faceted spacer bead
  - ½"-long faceted bead
  - Side-drilled accent bead

*Used in this project: 1 ball Dale of Norway's Tiur (100% pure new wool, 126yd/115m, 1.75oz/50g), color #4136.

**Bead amounts are approximate and may vary slightly in your own beadwork.

instructions

Foundation: Ch 2, turn.

Rnd 1: 6 sc in 2nd ch from hk, pm, do not turn.

Rnd 2: 2 sc in ea st - 12 sts.

Rnd 3: (Sc in next st, 2 sc in next st) rep 6 times - 18 sts.

Rnd 4: (Sc in next 2 sts, 2 sc in next st) rep 6 times - 24 sts.

Cont with 6 inc in ea rnd until you work a rep of (sc in the next 15 sts, 2 sc in the next st) for a total of 102 sts.

Work even with no inc for 15 rnds.

Weave in ends.

felting

Fold the bowl shape in half. Baste the opening closed with cotton cord. Felt in the washer, checking occasionally to see if the bag is completely felted. When the bag is felted to the desired texture, remove the basting cord, adjust to the finished shape, and let dry in a warm, dry place.

finishing

Fold the bag in half and sew the zipper in place. Sew the gimp over the zipper edge on the inside of the bag. Sew the gimp on the outside of the bag about ¼" from the top edge.

beading

Sew a beaded pull onto the zipper using the beads shown in the illustration.

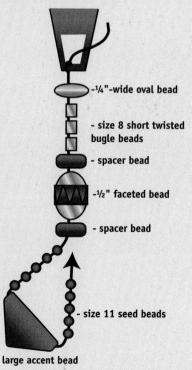

- ¼"-wide oval bead
- size 8 short twisted bugle beads
- spacer bead
- ½" faceted bead
- spacer bead
- size 11 seed beads

large accent bead

This bag, made of beautiful hand-dyed wool, presents a combination of techniques, from shaping and doily lace crochet to embroidery and tassel details that finish off the design. The long strap fits diagonally across your shoulder, and the piece is great to display near your favorite yarn basket.

leaf-embroidered tassel bag

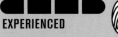
Finished Size Before Felting
10" x 15" not including tassel, with a 25"-long strap

Finished Size After Felting
8½" x 12" not including tassel, with a 35"-long strap

Stitches Used
ch
sl st
dc

Gauge in Double Crochet
14 sts and 8 rows = 4"

Note
When counting the sts in ea row, ch-3 and ch-4 count as a st, but when working in ea st to the last st, the ch-3 at the end of the row is not counted as a st.

materials

• 1 ball (250yd/230m) worsted weight wool yarn*
• Size H (5 mm) hook
• Tapestry needle
• 4" square thick cardboard

*Used in this project: 1 ball Mountain Colors 4/8's Wool (100% wool, 250yd/ 230m, 3.5oz/100g), color Olive.

Project before assembly and felting.

instructions

(Make one side through row 30, make other side through row 39.)

Foundation: Ch 4, turn.

Row 1: 2 dc in 4th ch from hk, turn.

Row 2: Ch 3, dc in next 2 sts, 2 dc in top of ch-4, turn - 5 sts.

Row 3: Ch 3, dc in ea st, dc in top of ch-3, turn - 6 sts.

Row 4 - 5: Rep row 3, turn - 7, 8 sts.

Row 6: Ch 3, 2 dc in 1st st, dc to last st, 2 dc in last st, dc in ch-3, turn - 11 sts.

Row 7 - 14: Rep row 6, turn - 14, 17, 20, 23, 26, 29, 32, 35 sts.

Row 15 - 30: Ch 3, dc in ea st across, turn.

flap

Row 31: Sl st in next 16 sts, sk 1, 6 dc in next st, sk 1, sl st in next 3 sts, turn.

Row 32: Sk sl st, 2 dc in ea of the 6 dc of the shell, sk 2, sl st in next st, turn.

Row 33: (Ch 3, sk 1, sl st) rep 6 times, sl st in next 2 sts, turn.

Row 34: Ch 1, dc in next ch-3 lp, ch 1, dc in same ch-3 lp, (ch 1, dc in next ch-3 lp, ch 1 dc in same ch-3 lp) rep 5 times, ch 1, sk 1, sl st in next 3 sts, turn.

Row 35: (Ch 1, sk ch-1 sp, 3 dc in next ch-1 sp) rep 6 times, ch 1, sk ch-1 sp, sl st in next 3 sts, turn.

Row 36: Ch 2, dc in ea of the next 3 dc, (ch 3, dc in ea of the next 3 dc) rep 5 times, ch 2, sk ch-1 sp, sk 1, sl st in next 3 sts, turn.

Row 37: Ch 2, (working in the top of the next 3 dc, dc in 1st st, 2 dc in 2nd st, dc in 3rd st, ch 3) rep 6 times, working only ch 2 at the end of the last rep, sk ch-2 sp, sk 1, sl st in next 3 sts, turn.

Row 38: (Ch 2, (working in the top of the next 4 dc (dc, ch 1) rep 4 times)), rep 6 times, ch 1, sk ch-2 sp, sk 1, sl st in next 3 sts, turn.

Row 39: Ch 1, (dc in next dc, (ch 4, sl st in 3rd ch from hk, ch 1, dc in next dc) rep 3 times)) rep 6 times, ch 1, sk ch-2 sp, sk 1, sl st in next st.

Weave in ends.

assembly

Sew the side seams together. Sew the strap ends to the bag at the top corners of the opening.

felting

Baste the opening of the bag closed with cotton cord. Baste the flap of the bag down over the front of the bag. Felt in the washer, checking occasionally to see if the bag is completely felted. When the bag is felted to the desired texture, remove the basting cord, adjust to the finished shape, and let dry in a warm, dry place.

embroidery

Using one strand of yarn and the tapestry needle, embroider the stems in stem stitch and the leaves in fly stitch following the illustrations below.

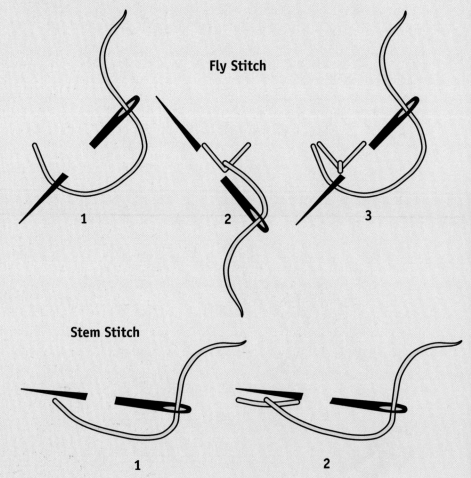

Fly Stitch

1   2   3

Stem Stitch

1   2

tassel

Wrap yarn around the cardboard 20 times.
With a 10" length of yarn, tie a tight
square knot around the wrapped yarn, as
in illustration below. Cut through all the
wraps at the opposite end of the knot.
Wrap a 12" length of yarn around the
folded end of the tassel as shown below
and tie the ends in a knot. Thread the
ends with a tapestry needle and hide
them in the tassel. Trim the ends of the
tassel so they are even and sew the tassel
to the bottom of the bag using the tails
of the 10" length of yarn.

**Tie these ends
into a knot.**

Cut at this end.

Wrap tassel.

chapter three

things to wear

One of the fun things about felting wearables is that you can custom shape them so the project really is made just for you. Slippers and hats benefit from putting them on for several minutes while they are still wet so they form to your shape, creating the perfect fit. While scarves and shawls don't need to be fitted, they are also fun felting projects because they are so easy to make, and you have the choice of felting them, or just leaving them as is, without felting. With three-dimensional decorative items, such as the flower projects, you can add a touch of color anywhere you choose.

This long, thin scarf is one step up from its eyelash-only cousin, since it will keep you wooly warm in addition to being fluffy and fun. If you make the wool section with twice as many rows, you will have a thicker scarf that flares at the edges and will keep you even warmer!

easy long eyelash scarf

EASY **MEDIUM** 4 **BULKY** 5

Finished Size Before Felting
3¼" x 68"

Finished Size After Felting
3" x 100"

Stitches Used
ch
sc
dc

Gauge in Double Crochet
16 sts and 8 rows = 4"

Project before (right) and after (left) felting.

materials

- 1 ball (233yd/209m)
  worsted weight wool yarn*
- 2 balls (57yd/52m)
  bulky weight eyelash yarn*
- Size H (5 mm) hook
- Tapestry needle

*Used in this project: 1 skein Lion
Brand Yarn's Monet (100% virgin
wool, 230yd/207m, 4oz/112g),
color #405 Peacock, and 2 balls
Lion Brand Fun Fur Prints (100%
polyester, 57yd/52m, 1.75oz/40g),
color #203 Indigo.

instructions

Foundation: Using wool yarn, ch
300, turn.

Row 1: Ch 3, dc in 4th ch from hk
and ea ch across, turn - 300 sts.

Row 2 - 3: Ch 3, dc in ea st
across, turn.

Row 4: Change to eyelash yarn
and rep row 2.

Row 5: Attach a new length of
eyelash yarn to the other end of
the foundation row and rep row 2.

Weave in ends.

felting

Felt in the washer, checking
occasionally to see if the
wool yarn is completely felted.
When the scarf is felted to the
desired texture, hang over a
hanger or chair and let dry in
a warm, dry place.

Here is a great scarf for experimenting with yarns. You can use a row or two of wool and a row or two of non-wool. You can add more yarn at the edges after felting or not even felt the project at all.

mixed media striped scarf

Finished Size Before Felting
3¼" x 68"

Finished Size After Felting
3½" x 80"

Stitches Used
ch
sc
dc

Gauge in Double Crochet
10 sts and 5 rows = 4"

Note
When counting sts in ea row, ch-2 and ch-3 count as a st.

materials

- 1 ball (122yd/110m) bulky weight suede novelty yarn*
- 1 ball (82yd/75m) bulky weight blended novelty yarn*
- 1 ball (110yd/100m) bulky weight ribbon novelty yarn*
- 1 ball (233yd/209m) worsted weight wool yarn*
- Size J (6 mm) hook

*Used in this project: 1 skein Lion Brand Yarn's Lion Suede (100% polyester, 122yd/110m, 3oz/85g), color #132 Olive, 1 ball Lion Brand Moonlight Mohair (35% mohair/30% acrylic/25% cotton/10% polyester metallic, 82yd/75m, 1.75oz/50g), color #201 Rain Forest, Lion Brand Yarn's Incredible (100% nylon, 110yd/100m, 1.75oz/50g), color #208 Copper Penny, and Lion Brand Yarn's Fishermen's Wool (100% virgin wool, 233yd/209m, 4oz/113g), color #98 Natural.

Project before felting.

instructions

Foundation: Using suede yarn, ch 175, turn.

Row 1: Ch 3, dc in 4th ch from hk and ea ch across - 175 sts.

Weave in ends.

Attach the wool and metallic blend yarns to the beg of the row. Holding both strands tog as 1, Ch 3, dc in ea st across, weave in ends.

Attach the suede yarn to the beg of the row just completed. Ch 1, sc in ea st across, weave in ends.

Rep these 2 rows on the other side of the dc suede so all the rows are worked from the right side of the scarf.

felting

Felt in the washer, checking occasionally to see if the wool yarn is completely felted and that the suede yarn is holding together. When the scarf is felted to the desired texture, adjust to the finished shape and let dry in a warm, dry place.

finishing

Attach the ribbon yarn to one corner of the scarf and work dc across that side of the scarf. Rep for the other side of the scarf. Weave in ends.

Cut 24 lengths (22") of ribbon and fold in half. Attach 12 lengths along each end of the scarf, two on the end of each double crochet and one on the end of the single crochets. Trim the ends of the fringe even, if necessary.

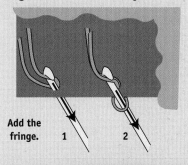

Add the fringe.   1   2

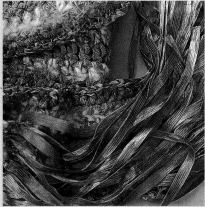

Here is another project that works just as well before or after felting. This stole is quick to make in the openwork stitch pattern, and it keeps you warm and toasty, especially after it is felted. The shell edging makes it easy to block, since you pull it to shape and put a pin in each point to hold it in place. This also ensures that the scalloped edging shows in the finished project.

netted stole

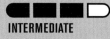

INTERMEDIATE **3 LIGHT**

Finished Size Before Felting
21" x 60"

Finished Size After Felting
18" x 58"

Stitches Used
ch
sl st
sc
dc

Gauge in Pattern Stitch
10 patt rep and 9 rows = 4"
Patt rep = ch 1, dc in ch sp

materials

- 2 hanks (525yd/483m) light worsted weight wool yarn*:
  - 1 navy
  - 1 plum
- Size H (5 mm) hook
- Cotton cord
- Tapestry needle

*Used in this project: 2 hanks Baabajoe's 8-ply Wool Pak Yarn (100% pure new New Zealand wool, 525yd/483m, 8oz/250g), colors Navy and Plum.

Project before felting.

Project after felting.

instructions
center section

Foundation: With plum yarn, ch 256 sts, turn.

Row 1: Ch 3, dc in 5th ch from hk, (ch 1, sk 1 ch, dc in next ch) rep 127 times, turn - 128 patt reps.

Row 2 - 31: Ch 3, (ch 1, dc in next ch sp) rep 128 times, turn.

Weave in ends.

border

Attach the navy yarn to a corner ch sp.

Row 1: (Ch 4, dc in same ch sp) twice, (ch 1, dc in next ch sp or end of row) rep to next corner, (ch 1 dc in same ch sp) twice, rep for ea side, ending with: ch 1, sl st in 3rd ch of ch-4.

Row 2: Sl st in next ch sp, ch 4, dc in same ch sp, ch 1, dc in next ch sp, ch 1, dc in same ch sp, (ch 1, dc in next ch sp) rep to next corner, work 2 patt reps in 2 corner sts, rep patt around, ch 1, sl st in 3rd ch of ch-4.

Row 3: Sl st in next 3 sts. You will be in the corner ch sp. Ch 4, dc in same ch sp, (ch 1, dc in same ch sp), work in patt to next corner, work 3 patt reps in corner ch sp, cont in

patt to beg of row, ending with ch 1, sl st in 3rd ch of ch-4.

Rep row 2 -3 twice more.

Rep row 2.

picot edge

Sl st in the next ch sp, ch 3, (3 dc, ch 2, 4 dc) in the same ch sp, ch 2, sk 1 ch sp, sc in next ch sp, ch 2, sk next ch sp, ((4 dc, ch 2, 4 dc) in the next ch sp, ch 2, sk 1 ch sp, sc in next ch sp, ch 2, sk next ch sp) rep around, sl st in top of ch-3.

Weave in ends.

felting

Fold the wrap in half and baste the edges together with cotton cord. Felt in the washer, checking occasionally to see if the wrap is completely felted. When the wrap is felted to the desired texture, remove the basting cord, adjust to the finished shape, and let dry in a warm, dry place.

Fold as shown and baste the edges.

Felted hats are always fun to make because it's such a transformation from the floppy bag shape to the final fitted hat. You also have a lot of room for adjustments when forming your hat into its final shape. By basting the base of the brim the final hat size, you can have some control over how much your hat will shrink in the felting process. Be sure to check your hat often while it's felting so it doesn't felt too small to fit!

gardening hat

INTERMEDIATE  **3 LIGHT**

Finished Size Before Felting
15" tall x 17" diameter

Finished Size After Felting
To fit 21" head circumference with a 3" brim

Stitches Used
ch
hdc
sl st

Gauge in Double Crochet
15 sts and 7 rows = 4"

Note
When counting sts in ea row, ch-2 and ch-3 count as a st.

materials
- 1 hank (525yd/483m) light worsted weight wool yarn*
- Size H (5 mm) hook
- Cotton cord
- Tapestry needle

*Used in this project: 1 hank Baabajoe's 8-ply Wool Pak Yarn (100% pure new New Zealand wool, 525yd/483m, 8oz/250g), color Oatmeal.

Project after felting.

instructions

Foundation: Ch 4, turn.

Row 1: 9 dc in 4th ch from hk, sl st in top of ch-4, do not turn - 10 sts.

Row 2: Ch 3, 2 dc in next 9 sts, dc in base of ch-3, sl st in top of ch-3 - 20 sts.

Row 3: Ch 3, (dc in next st, 2 dc in next st) rep 9 times, dc in next st, dc in base of ch-3, sl st in top of ch-3 - 30 sts.

Row 4: Ch 3, (dc in next 2 sts, 2 dc in next st) rep 9 times, dc in next 2 sts, dc in base of ch-3, sl st in top of ch-3 - 40 sts.

Row 5: Ch 3, (dc in next 3 sts, 2 dc in next st) rep 9 times, dc in next 3 sts, dc in base of ch-3, sl st in top of ch-3 - 50 sts.

Row 6: Ch 3, (dc in next 4 sts, 2 dc in next st) rep 9 times, dc in next 4 sts, dc in base of ch-3, sl st in top of ch-3 - 60 sts.

Row 7 - 9: Cont inc as in rows 3 - 6 until you (dc in next 7 sts, 2 dc in next st) and have 90 sts after row 9.

Row 10 - 22: Ch 3, dc in ea st around, sl st in top of ch-3.

Row 23: Ch 3, (dc in next 4 sts, 2 dc in next st) rep 17 times, dc in next 4 sts, dc in base of ch-3, sl st in top of ch-3 - 108 sts.

Row 24 - 26: Rep row 10.

Row 27: Ch 3, (dc in next 9 sts, 2 dc in next st) rep 10 times, dc in next 7 sts, join to top of ch-3 - 118 sts.

Row 28: Rep row 10.

Row 29: Ch 3, (dc in next 9 sts, 2 dc in next st) rep 11 times, dc in next 7 sts, sl st in top of ch-3 - 129 sts.

Row 30 - 31: Rep row 10.

Weave in ends.

felting

Baste along the brim, pull the basting thread to the finished hat size and tie in a square knot. Felt the hat in the washer, checking often to see if the hat is the correct size. When felted to the desired size, try on the hat, carefully remove from washer, shape the top and tbrim, and let dry in a warm, dry place.

Baste to size along the brim edge.

Here is an afternoon project that transforms into a wonderful, useful pair of cozy slippers. It would be fun to make them as a gift, but let the recipient felt them down to the perfect size and shape for their own feet. Offer to be on hand for the felting session, just to make sure they don't get felted too small!

quick and easy shape-to-fit slippers

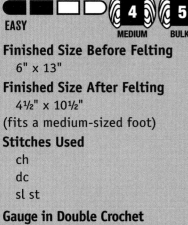

EASY **MEDIUM** **BULKY** 4 5

Finished Size Before Felting
6" x 13"

Finished Size After Felting
4½" x 10½"
(fits a medium-sized foot)

Stitches Used
ch
dc
sl st

Gauge in Double Crochet
(holding 2 strands wool and 1
strand novelty yarn tog as 1)
7 sts and 4 rows = 4"

materials

- 2 balls (223yd/204m)
  worsted weight wool yarn*
- 2 balls (47yd/43m)
  bulky weight novelty yarn*
- Size N (10mm) hook
- Tapestry needle

*Used in this project: 2 balls Patons'
Classic Wool Merino (100% pure new
wool, 223yd/204m, 3.5oz/100g), color
#77023 Camel and 2 balls Patons'
Allure (100% nylon, 47yd/43m,
1.75oz/50g), color #4011 Sable.

Project before felting.

instructions

Foundation: Using 2 strands wool
and 1 strand novelty yarn held tog
as 1 throughout, ch 4, turn.

Row 1: 9 dc in 4th ch from hk, sl
st in top of ch-4.

Row 2: Ch 3, 2 dc in ea st, sl st in
top of ch-3 - 18 sts.

Row 3 - 8: Ch 3, dc in ea st, sl st
in top of ch-3.

Row 9 - 12: Ch 3, dc in next 13
sts, turn.

Cut the three strands of yarn to
12", thread with tapestry needle,
and pass through lp on hk. Fold
last row in half and seam tog with
12" tail.

Weave in ends.

felting

Fold the opening in half and baste
together with cotton cord. Felt in
the washer, checking occasionally
to see if the slippers are felted to
your foot size. When the slippers
are felted to the desired size and
texture, remove the basting cord,
adjust to the finished shape by
trying on for several minutes,
then carefully take them off and
let dry in a warm, dry place.

Project after felting.

A more elegant alternative to the fuzzy slippers on the previous page, these slippers have the added detail of a loose and fluffy ankle covering so you are protected from drafts on cool mornings. They shrink to fit, just like their fluffy counterparts, and the fluffy collar stays loose at your ankles like socks that have been pushed down from your calf.

novelty yarn-topped slippers

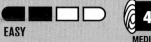

EASY

4 MEDIUM

Finished Size Before Felting
5½" x 11"

Finished Size After Felting
Fits a medium-sized foot

Stitches Used
ch
hdc
dc

Gauge in Half Double Crochet
14 sts and 10 rows = 4"

Project before felting.

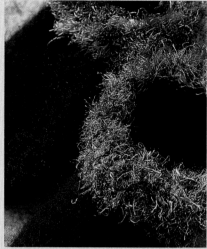
Project after felting.

materials

- 1 ball (223yd/204m) worsted weight wool yarn*
- 1 ball (77yd/70m) bulky weight novelty yarn*
- Size H (5 mm) hook
- Tapestry needle
- Stitch marker

*Used in this project: 1 ball Patons' Classic Wool Merino (100% pure new wool, 223yd/204m, 3.5oz/100g), color #226 Black and 1 ball Patons' Cha Cha (100% nylon, 77yd/70m, 1.75oz/50g), color #2006 Jazz.

instructions
slipper

Foundation: Using wool yarn, ch 12, turn.

Row 1: Ch 2, hdc in back half of the 3rd ch from hk, and ea ch to the last ch, 5 hdc in the last ch, working on the other side of the sts, hdc in the next 10 sts, 5 hdc in the 1st st, pm, do not turn - 31 sts.

Row 2: Hdc in next 13 sts, 2 hdc in next 3 sts, hdc in next 12 sts, 2 hdc in next 3 sts - 37 sts.

Row 3 - 19: Work even.

Row 20: Fold crocheting in half so it lies flat and mark the top row about one-third from the right side. Hdc in ea st until you get to marker, turn.

Row 21: Ch 2, hdc in ea st to the last 7 sts, turn.

Row 22 - 30: Ch 2, hdc in ea st, turn.

Fold the last row in half, beg at the corners and working towards the middle of the row, sc across working into both ends held tog as 1.

Weave in ends.

cuff

Attach the novelty yarn to the heel end of the foot opening.

Rnd 1: Ch 2, 2 dc in the end of ea row and dc in ea st, rep until you complete the opening circle.

Rnd 2: Dc in or between ea st around.

Weave in end.

felting

Felt in the washer, checking often to make sure the slippers don't felt too small. When the slippers are close to the correct size, try them on and wear for several minutes, then carefully remove them and let dry in a warm, dry place.

A great thing about felting is that once your crocheting is felted, you can cut it up and make it into anything you can think of! These fun flower designs are quickly worked up from felted fabric, and then thrown in the washer again to soften the cut edges even more. Use them on any of the projects in this section or the next to liven up your wardrobe or home décor.

flowers to embellish anything

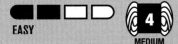

EASY

4 MEDIUM

Finished Size Before Felting
11½" x 11" (two tubes with ends sewn tog, in green and pink)

Finished Size After Felting
3½" x 2½" rose with 4½"-long leaves

Stitches Used
ch
dc

Gauge in Double Crochet
15 sts and 8 rows = 4"

Note
When counting sts in ea row, ch-2 and ch-3 count as a st.

materials

- 3 balls (223yd/204m) worsted weight wool yarn*
  - 2 pink
  - 1 green
- Size H (5 mm) hook
- Cotton cord
- Tapestry needle
- Sewing needle and thread to match yarn color
- Sewing scissors
- Sewing machine (optional)

*Used in this project: 3 balls Patons' Classic Wool Merino (100% pure new wool, 223yd/204m, 3.5oz/100g): 2 balls in color #233 Blush and 1 ball in color #222 Sage.

Project before felting.

Project after felting.

instructions

(Make one in green and one in pink.)

Foundation: Ch 90.

Rnd 1: Join into a circle by dc in the back half of the 1st ch, being careful to keep the ch untwisted, dc in the back half of ea ch around.

Cont with dc in ea st until you run out of yarn.

Weave in ends.

felting

Baste top and bottom openings closed with cotton cord. Felt in the washer, checking occasionally until yarn is completely felted. Remove the basting stitches, adjust to rectangle shape and let dry in a warm, dry place

making the flower

Cut the pink felt into a long triangle, 15" long and 3" tall at one corner. Round the 3" end.

Beginning at the 3" end, roll the triangle up into a tight coil so the bottom is all the same level and the top is tall in the center.

Sew the bottom together with the sewing needle and thread.

Cut three petal shapes from the pink felt using the pattern on the next page.

Sew petals to the side of the flower center, overlapping each petal as you attach it.

Cut the leaf shape from the green felt, using the leaf pattern on the next page.

Optional: Machine-stitch lines in the leaf to simulate veins.

Sew the leaf to the bottom of the flower.

Felt again, if desired, to soften the cut edges of the flower.

flowers to embellish anything

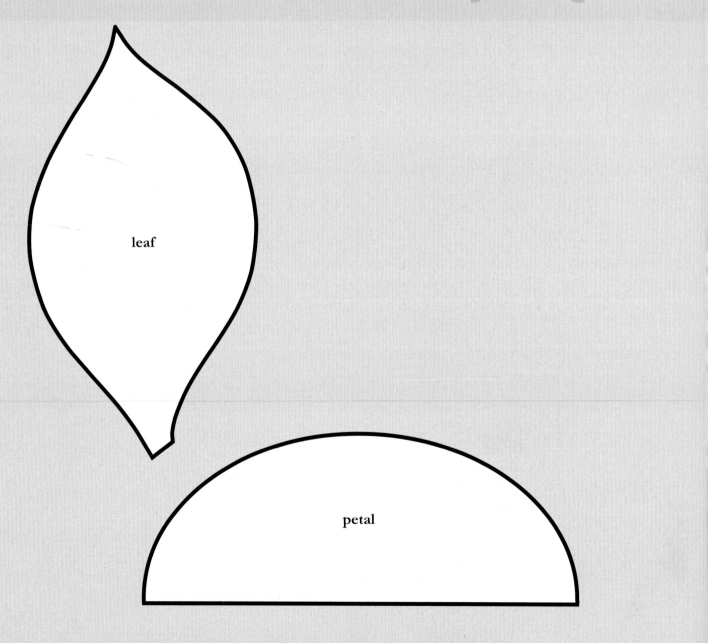

leaf

petal

chapter four

home decorating

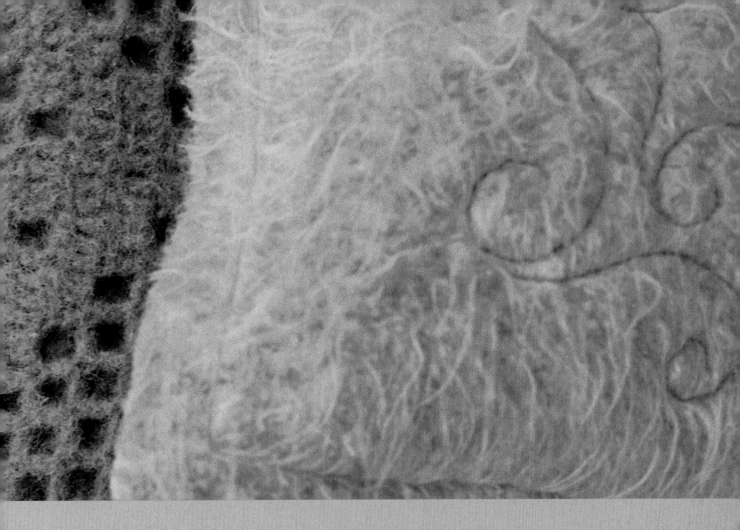

Home decorating with felted crochet opens up a lot of possibilities, since you have the option of cutting and sewing anything from pillows to placemats. Rugs and blankets allow you to try your hand at more involved projects that can add to your décor and warm your family at the same time.

The yarn makes this simple pattern shine. You could make a set of placemats, and each would be unique in this color transitioning yarn. The curling edge of the placemat flattens out in the felting process. Because this yarn is a blend, it shows how the project only partially felts.

placemat and coaster

EASY · **MEDIUM** 4

Finished Size Before Felting
(with edge unrolled flat)
  13½" x 16½" (placemat)
  4" diameter (coaster)

Finished Size After Felting
  11" x 13" (placemat)
  3¾" diameter (coaster)

Stitches Used
  ch
  sc

Gauge in Single Crochet
  17 sts and 18 rows = 4"

materials

- 2 balls (110yd/101m) worsted weight wool blend yarn*
- Size H (5 mm) hook
- Tapestry needle
- Stitch marker

*Used in this project: 2 balls Noro's (45% silk, 45% mohair, 10% lambswool, 110yd/101m, 1.75oz/ 50g), one each of color #8 and #86.

Project before felting.

Project after felting.

instructions

placemat

Foundation: Ch 12, turn.

Rnd 1: Sc in back half of 2nd ch from hk and ea ch to last ch, 3 sc in back half of last ch, working back up the other side of the ch, sc in the other half of ea ch to the 1st ch, 3 sc in the 1st ch, pm, do not turn.

Rem rnds: Work sc in ea st, making 2 sc 3 times at ea end of the piece, by either making the 2 sc in the center of the previous 2 sc, or by changing the placement by 2 or 3 sts so it doesn't make a noticeable patt. Cont until piece is approx 9" x 11", then work without inc until piece measures approx 13½" x 16½".

Weave in ends.

coaster

Foundation: Ch 2, turn.

Rnd 1: 6 sc in 2nd ch from hk, pm, do not turn.

Rnd 2: 2 sc in ea st - 12 sts.

Rnd 3: (Sc in next st, 2 sc in next st) rep 6 times - 18 sts.

Rnd 4: (Sc in next 2 sts, 2 sc in next st) rep 6 times - 24 sts.

Cont with 6 inc in ea rnd until you work a rep of (sc in the next 9 sts, 2 sc in the next st) for a total of 66 sts.

Weave in ends.

felting

Felt in the washer, checking occasionally to see if the pieces are completely felted. When the pieces are felted to the desired texture, adjust to the finished shape and let dry in a warm, dry place.

Working with this thick roving yarn in a smaller hook than you normally would makes a stiff bowl to begin with. Felting it makes it even stronger, creating the perfect soft furnishing bowl to hold your favorite yarn or thread, or just to have near your crochet basket at home.

stiff yarn bowl

EASY

SUPER BULKY 6

Finished Size Before Felting
13" diameter

Finished Size After Felting
8" diameter

Stitches Used
ch

hdc

sl st

Gauge in Double Crochet
12 sts and 7 rows = 4"

Note
When counting sts in ea row, ch-2 and ch-3 count as a st.

materials

- 1 ball (78yd/71m) bulky weight wool yarn*
- Size I (5.5 mm) hook

*Used in this project: 1 ball Patons' Up Country (100% wool, 78yd/71m, 3.5oz/100g), color #80953 Ice Blue.

Project before felting.

Project after felting.

instructions

Foundation: Ch 4, turn.

Row 1: 9 dc in 4th ch from hk, sl st in top of ch-4, do not turn.

Row 2: Ch 3, 2 dc in ea st and 1 dc base of ch-3, sl st in top of ch-3 - 20 sts.

Row 3: Ch 3, (dc in next st, 2 dc in next st) rep 9 times, dc in next st, dc in base of ch-3, sl st in top of ch-3 - 30 sts.

Row 4: Ch 3, (dc in next 2 sts, 2 dc in next st) rep 9 times, dc in next 2 sts, dc in base of ch-3, sl st in top of ch-3 - 40 sts.

Row 5: Ch 3, (dc in next 3 sts, 2 dc in next st) rep 9 times, dc in next 3 sts, dc in base of ch-3, sl st in top of ch-3 - 50 sts.

Row 6: Ch 3, (dc in next 4 sts, 2 dc in next st) rep 9 times, dc in next 4 sts, dc in base of ch-3, sl st in top of ch-3 - 60 sts.

Row 7: Ch 3, (dc in next 5 sts, 2 dc in next st) rep 9 times, dc in next 5 sts, dc in base of ch-3, sl st in top of ch-3 - 70 sts.

Row 8 - 10: Work even for 3 rows.

Row 11: Ch 1, (sc in next 6 sts, sk next st) rep 10 times, sl st in ch-1.

Weave in ends.

felting

Felt in the washer, checking occasionally to see if the bowl is completely felted. When the bowl is felted to the desired texture, adjust to the finished shape and let dry in a warm, dry place.

Felted fabric is a wonderful surface to show off machine embroidery designs. The thick, furry texture of this mohair blend yarn accentuates the machine-stitched pattern and is a quick and easy home decorating project to add your personal touch.

machine-quilted pillow

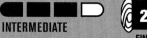

INTERMEDIATE

2 FINE

Finished Size Before Felting
18½" x 24"

Finished Project
12" square

Stitches Used
ch
dc

Gauge in Double Crochet
(with 2 strands yarn held
tog as 1)
13 sts and 7 rows = 4"

Project before felting.

materials

- 6 balls (126yd/115m)
  fine weight wool yarn*:
    - 3 white
    - 3 blue
- Size I (5.5 mm) hook
- Cotton cord
- Tapestry needle
- 13" square backing fabric
- 12" pillow form
- Sewing machine and
  thread to match fabric and yarn
- Sewing needle and
  thread to match fabric
- Freezer paper
- Pencil
- Iron
- Ironing board

*Used in this project: 6 balls Dale of
Norway's Tiur (100% pure new wool,
126yd/115m, 1.75oz/50g), 3 in color
#0020 Off White, and 3 in color #6222
Light Blue.

instructions

Foundation: Holding 1 strand of
ea color yarn tog as 1 throughout,
ch 60, turn.

Row 1: Ch 3, dc in 4th ch from hk
and ea ch across, turn - 60 sts.

Row 2 - 43: Ch 3, dc in ea st
across, turn.

Weave in ends.

felting

Fold the square in half and
baste the edges together with
cotton cord. Felt in the washer,
checking occasionally to see if
it is completely felted. When the
square is felted to the desired
texture, remove the basting cord,
adjust to finished shape, and let
dry in a warm, dry place.

(continued)

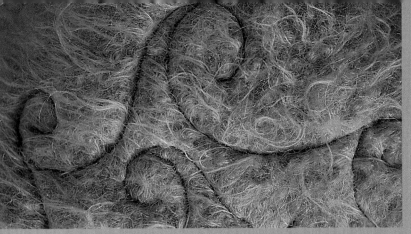

Project after felting.

machine-quilted pillow

finishing

Trace the pattern onto freezer paper and iron it to the felted surface.

Machine-stitch along the pattern lines. Tear the paper away from the stitching.

Fold the raw edges of the fabric square under ½".

Topstitch the fabric to the felt about ¼" from the edges, leaving one side open to insert the pillow form.

Topstitch on the felt only on the unsewn side so it has the same stitching line along the edge as the rest of the sides.

Insert the pillow form in the pillow and hand-sew the opening shut.

Rotate pattern to create complete design.

Machine-stitch along the pattern lines.　　center

Filet netting is a wonderful crochet technique to work in felting projects, since it makes the solid sections of double crochet blend into a whole, showing off the design more clearly, rather than having it fade away. Your choice of background fabric for this pillow is critical for the design to show, so be sure to find a dark contrast to your yarn choice.

filet netted pillow

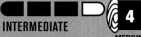

INTERMEDIATE

MEDIUM 4

Finished Size Before Felting
22" x 22"

Finished Size After Felting
20" square

Stitches Used
ch
dc

Gauge in Double Crochet
16 sts and 7 rows = 4"

Note
When counting sts in ea row, ch-2 and ch-3 count as a st.

Project before felting.

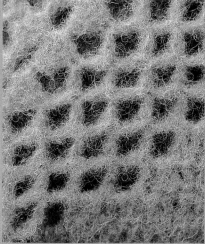
Project after felting.

materials

- 2 balls (200yd/184m) worsted weight wool yarn*
- Size H (5 mm) hook
- Cotton cord
- Tapestry needle
- 2 squares (20") fabric
- Sewing machine and thread to match fabric
- 20" square pillow form
- Iron
- Ironing board
- Straight pins

*Used in this project: 2 balls Harrisville Designs New England Knitter's Highland (100% wool, 200yd/184m, 3.5oz/100g), color #12 Seagreen.

instructions

Follow the line-by-line instructions below or the graphed patt, page 83. For the graphed patt, ea solid square is 4 dc, and ea open square is ch 2. Adjoining squares share 1 st. The black dot shows where to beg.

Foundation: Ch 4, turn.

Row 1: 2 dc in 4th ch from hk, (ch 2, 3 dc in same 4th ch from hk) rep 3 times, ch 2, sl st in top of ch-4.

Row 2: Ch 3, (ch 2, (3 dc, ch 2, 3 dc) in next ch sp) rep 3 times, ch 2, (3 dc, ch 2, 2 dc) in next ch sp, sl st in 3rd ch of ch-5.

Row 3: Ch 5, (dc in 1st st of next CL, ch 2, (3 dc, ch 2, 3 dc) in next ch sp, ch 2, dc in last st of next CL, ch 2) rep 4 times except on last rep omit last dc and ch 2, sl st in 3rd ch of ch-5.

Row 4: Ch 5, (dc in next dc, ch 2, dc in 1st st of next CL, ch 2, (3 dc, ch 2, 3 dc) in next ch sp, ch 2, dc in last st of next CL, ch 2, dc in next dc, ch 2) rep 4 times except on last rep omit last dc and ch 2, sl st in 3rd ch of ch-5.

Row 5: Ch 3, [2 dc in next ch sp, dc in next dc, ch 2, dc in next dc, ch 2, dc in first st of next CL, ch 2, (3 dc, ch 2, 3 dc) in next ch sp, ch 2, dc in last st of next CL, ch 2, dc in next dc, ch 2, dc in next dc] rep 4 times, except omit the last dc on the last dc, sl st in the top of ch-3.

Row 6: Ch 5, dc in last st of dc group, 2 dc in ch sp, dc in next dc, (ch 2, dc in next dc) twice, ch 2, (3 dc, ch 2, 3 dc) in next ch sp, [ch 2, dc in last st of next CL, (ch 2, dc in next dc) twice, 2 dc in next ch sp, dc in next dc, ch 2, dc in last st of dc group, 2 dc in next ch sp, dc in next dc, (ch 2, dc in next dc) twice, ch 2, (3 dc, ch 2, 3 dc) in next ch sp] rep 3 times, ch 2 dc in last st of next CL, (ch 2, dc in next dc) twice, 2 dc in next ch sp, sl st in 3rd ch of ch-5.

Row 7: Ch 3, 2 dc in next ch sp, dc in next dc, ch 2, dc in last st of next dc group, (ch 2, dc in next dc) rep 3 times, ch 2, (3 dc, ch 2, 3 dc) in next ch sp, [ch 2, dc in last st of next CL, (ch 2, dc in next dc) rep 3 times, ch 2 dc in last st of next dc group, 2 dc in next ch sp, dc in next dc, ch 2, dc in last st of next dc group, (ch 2, dc in next dc) rep 3 times, ch 2, (3 dc, ch 2, 3 dc) in next ch sp] rep 3 times, ch 2, dc in last st of next CL, (ch 2, dc in next dc) rep 3 times, ch 2, sl st in top of ch-3.

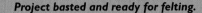

Project basted and ready for felting.

filet netted pillow

Row 8: Ch 3, dc in next 3 dc, (ch 2, dc in next dc) rep 5 times, ch 2, (3 dc, ch 2, 3 dc) in next ch sp, [ch 2, dc in last st of next CL, (ch 2, dc in next dc) rep 5 times, dc in next 3 dc, (ch 2, dc in next dc) rep 5 times, ch 2, (3 dc, ch 2, 3 dc) in next ch sp] rep 3 times, ch 2, dc in last st of next CL, (ch 2, dc in next dc) rep 4 times, ch 2, sl st in top of ch-3.

Row 9: Ch 3, dc in next 3 dc, 2 dc in next ch sp, dc in next dc, (ch 2, dc in next dc) rep 5 times, ch 2, (3 dc, ch 2, 3 dc) in next ch sp, [ch 2, dc in last st of next CL, (ch 2, dc in next dc) rep 5 times, 2 dc in next ch sp, dc in next 4 dc, 2 dc in next ch sp, dc in next dc, (ch 2, dc in next dc) rep 5 times, ch 2, (3 dc, ch 2, 3 dc) in next ch sp] rep 3 times, ch 2, dc in last dc of next CL, (ch 2, dc in next dc) rep 5 times, 2 dc in next ch sp, sl st in top of ch-3.

Row 10: Ch 3, dc in next 6 dc, 2 dc in next ch sp, dc in next dc, (ch 2, dc in next dc) rep 5 times, ch 2, (3 dc, ch 2, 3 dc) in next ch

sp, [ch 2, dc in last st of next CL, (ch 2, dc in next dc) rep 5 times, 2 dc in next ch sp, dc in next 10 dc, 2 dc in next ch sp, dc in next dc, (ch 2, dc in next dc) rep 5 times, ch 2, (3 dc, ch 2, 3 dc) in next ch sp], rep 3 times, ch 2, dc in last dc of next CL, (ch 2, dc in next dc) rep 5 times, 2 dc in next ch sp, dc in next 3 dc, sl st in top of ch-3.

Row 11: Ch 3, dc in next 3 sts, ch 2, sk 2, dc in next 4 sts, 2 dc in next ch sp, dc in next dc, (ch 2, dc in next dc) rep 5 times, ch 2, (3 dc, ch 2, 3 dc) in next ch sp, [ch 2, dc in last st of next CL, (ch 2, dc in next dc) rep 5 times, 2 dc in next ch sp, dc in next 4 dc, ch 2, sk 2, dc in next 4 dc, ch 2, sk 2, dc in next 4 dc, 2 dc in next ch sp, dc in next dc, (ch 2, dc in next dc) rep 5 times, ch 2, (3 dc, ch 2, 3 dc) in next ch sp] rep 3 times, ch 2 dc in last st of next CL, (ch 2, dc in next dc) rep 5 times, 2 dc in next ch sp, dc in next 4 dc, ch 2, sl st in top of ch-3.

Row 12: Ch 3, dc in next 3 sts, ch

2, dc in next st, ch 2, sk 2, dc in next 4 sts, (2 dc in next ch sp, dc in next dc) twice, (ch 2, dc in next dc) rep 4 times, ch 2 (3 dc, ch 2, 3 dc) in next ch sp, [ch 2, dc in last st of next CL, (ch 2, dc in next dc) rep 4 times, (2 dc in next ch sp, dc in next dc) twice, dc in next 3 dc, (ch 2, sk 2 ch or dc, dc in next dc) twice, dc in next 3 sts, (ch 2, sk 2 ch or dc, dc in next dc) twice, dc in next 3 dc, (2 dc in next ch sp, dc in next dc) twice, (ch 2 dc in next dc) rep 4 times, ch 2 (3 dc, ch 2, 3 dc) in next ch sp], ch 2, dc in last st of next CL, (ch 2, dc in next dc) rep 4 times, (2 dc in next ch sp, dc in next dc) twice, dc in next 3 sts, ch 2, sk 2, dc in next dc, ch 2, sl st in top of ch-3.

Row 13: Ch 3, dc in next 3 sts, (ch 2, dc in next dc) twice, dc in next 9 dc, 2 dc in next ch sp, dc in next dc, (ch 2, dc in next dc) rep 4 times, ch 2, (3 dc, ch 2, 3 dc) in next ch sp, [ch 2, dc in last st of next CL, (ch 2 dc in next dc) rep 4 times, 2 dc in next ch sp, dc in next 10 sts, (ch 2, dc in next dc) twice, dc in next 3 sts, (ch 2, dc in next dc) twice, dc in next 9 sts, 2 dc in next ch sp, dc in next dc, (ch 2, dc in next dc) rep 4 times, ch 2, (3 dc, ch 2, 3 dc) in next ch sp], rep 3 times, ch 2, dc in last st of next CL, (ch 2, dc in next dc) rep 4 times, 2 dc in next ch sp, dc in next 10 sts, ch 2, dc in next dc, ch 2, sl st in top of ch-3.

Row 14: Ch 3, dc in next 3 dc, 2 dc in next ch sp, dc in next dc, ch 2, dc in next dc, ch 2, sk 2, dc in next 10 sts, (ch 2, dc in next dc) rep 5 times, ch 2, (3 dc, ch 2, 3 dc) in next ch sp, [ch 2, dc in last st of next CL, (ch 2 dc in next dc) rep 5 times, dc in next 9 sts, (ch 2, sk 2 ch or dc, dc in next dc) twice, 2 dc in next ch sp, dc in next 4 sts, 2 dc in next ch sp, dc in next dc, (ch 2, sk 2 ch or dc, dc in next dc) twice, dc in next 9 sts, (ch 2, dc in next dc) rep 5 times, ch 2, (3 dc, ch 2, 3 dc) in next ch sp] rep 3 times, ch 2, dc in last st of next CL, (ch 2 dc in next dc) rep 5 times, dc in next 9 sts, (ch 2, sk 2 ch or dc, dc in next dc) twice, 2 dc in next ch sp, sl st in top of ch-3.

Row 15: Ch 3, dc in next 6 sts, (ch 2, dc in next dc) twice, ch 2, sk 2, dc in next 7 sts, (ch 2, dc in next dc) rep 6 times, ch 2, (3 dc, ch 2, 3 dc) in next ch sp, [ch 2, dc in last st of next CL, (ch 2 dc in next dc) rep 6 times, dc in next 6 sts, ch 2, sk 2, dc in next dc, (ch 2, dc in next dc) twice, dc in next 9 sts, (ch 2, dc in next dc) twice, ch 2, sk 2, dc in next 7 sts (ch 2, dc in next dc) rep 6 times, ch 2, (3 dc, ch 2, 3 dc) in next ch sp] rep 3 times, ch 2, dc in last st of next CL, (ch 2 dc in next dc) rep 6 times, dc in next 6 sts, ch 2, sk 2, dc in next dc, (ch 2, dc in next dc) twice, dc in next 2 sts, sl st in top of ch-3.

Row 16: Ch 3, dc in next 3 sts, ch 2, sk 2, dc in next dc, 2 dc in next ch sp, dc in next dc, (ch 2, dc in next dc) twice, ch 2, sk 2, dc in next 4 dc, (ch 2, dc in next dc) rep 7 times, ch 2, (3 dc, ch 2, 3 dc) in next ch sp, [ch 2, dc in last st of next CL, (ch 2 dc in next dc) rep 7 times, dc in next 3 sts, ch 2, sk 2, dc in next st, (ch 2, dc in next dc) twice, 2 dc in next ch sp, dc in next dc, ch 2 sk 2, dc in next 4 sts, ch 2, sk 2, dc in next dc, 2 dc in next ch sp, dc in next dc, (ch 2, dc in next dc) twice, ch 2, sk 2, dc in next 4 sts, (ch 2, dc in next dc) rep 7 times, ch 2, (3 dc, ch 2, 3 dc) in next ch sp] rep 3 times, ch 2, dc in last st of next CL, (ch 2 dc in next dc) rep 7 times, dc in next 3 sts, ch 2, sk 2, dc in next st, (ch 2, dc in next dc) twice, 2 dc in next ch sp, dc in next dc, ch 2, sl st in top of ch-3.

Row 17: Ch 5, sk 2, dc in next dc, 2 dc in ch sp, dc in next dc, ch 2, sk 2, dc in next dc, (ch 2, dc in next dc) rep 3 times, dc in next 3 sts, (ch 2, dc in next dc) rep 8 times, ch 2, (3 dc, ch 2, 3 dc) in next ch sp, [ch 2, dc in last st of next CL, (ch 2 dc in next dc) rep 8 times, dc in next 3 sts, (ch 2, dc in next dc) rep 3 times, ch 2, sk 2, dc in next dc, 2 dc in next ch sp, dc in next dc, ch 2, sk 2, dc in next dc, 2 dc in next ch sp, dc in next dc, ch 2, sk 2, dc in next dc, (ch 2, dc in next dc) rep 3 times, dc in next 3 dc, (ch 2, dc in next dc) rep 8 times, ch 2, (3 dc, ch 2, 3 dc) in next ch sp] rep 3 times, ch 2, dc in last st of next CL, (ch 2 dc in next dc) rep 8 times, dc in next 3 sts, (ch 2, dc in next dc) rep 3 times, ch 2, sk 2, dc in next dc, 2 dc in next ch sp, sl st in top of ch-3.

Weave in ends.

felting

Fold the square into a smaller square by bringing the four points to the center and baste the edges together with cotton cord. Felt in the washer, checking occasionally to see if it is completely felted. When the square is felted to the desired texture, remove the basting cord, adjust to the finished shape and let dry in a warm, dry place.

assembly

Pin the two fabric squares, right sides together and sew a ½" seam, leaving about 15" open on one side to insert the pillow form.

Trim the corners and turn the casing right-side out.

Press flat, pressing the 15"-opening edges ½" to the inside.

Pin the casing to the back of the felted crochet so that the casing edge is at the beginning of the second-to-last row of crocheting.

Topstitch through the end of the third-to-last row of crocheting, and the edge of the pillow casing, stitching only through the two top layers on the 15" opening.

Insert the pillow form and hand-sew the 15" opening closed.

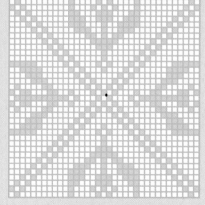

Graphed pattern.

My son took this blanket before I finished it, and was a little apprehensive about me throwing it in the washer to felt. He thought it was just fine the way it was. I think he was right; this project doesn't need to be felted, but in the felting, the wool softens a little and the eyelash yarn fluffs out so the blanket ends up more warm and soft than it was before felting. My son tried it out in front of the TV after it was felted and was just as happy with it as he was before it was felted.

fuzzy striped blanket

Finished Size Before Felting
51" x 57"

Finished Size After Felting
44" x 52"

Stitches Used
ch
dc

Gauge in Double Crochet (using wool yarn)
14 sts and 7 rows = 4"

Note

When counting sts in ea row, ch-3 does not count as a st.

When working into the novelty yarn, it is sometimes difficult to find where to insert the hk. Sometimes working between the stitches is easier than trying to find the top of the st.

materials

- 4 balls (465yd/425m) worsted weight wool yarn*
- 16 balls (57yd/52m) eyelash novelty yarn*:
  - 9 multicolored neutrals
  - 5 brown
  - 2 cream
- Size H (5 mm) hook

*Used in this project: 4 skeins Lion Brand Yarn's Fishermen's Wool (100% virgin wool, 465yd/425m, 8oz/227g), color #98 Natural, and 16 balls Lion Brand Fun Fur Prints (100% polyester, 57yd/52m, 1.75oz/40g), 9 in color #205 Sandstone, 5 in color #126 Chocolate and 2 in color #124 Champagne.

Project before felting.

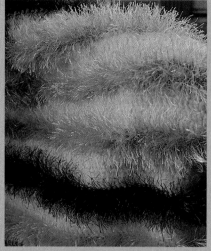

Project after felting.

instructions

Foundation: Using the wool yarn, ch 170, turn.

Row 1: Ch 3, dc in 4th ch from hk and ea ch across, turn - 170 dc.

Row 2-4: Ch 3, dc in ea st across, turn.

Row 5: Change to multicolored novelty yarn, ch 3, dc in ea st across, turn.

Row 6: Ch 3, dc in ea st, or between ea st across, turn.

Row 7: Change to wool yarn, ch 3, dc in ea st, or between ea st, across, turn.

Row 8-10: Ch 3, dc in ea st across, turn.

Rep rows 5-10, working the next rep with multicolored novelty yarn, then following the color sequence below 3 times, working only 2 reps of multicolored novelty yarn on the last rep.

- brown novelty yarn once
- cream novelty yarn once
- brown novelty yarn once
- multicolored novelty yarn 3 times

Using multicolored novelty yarn, work 2 rows of dc around the edges of the blanket, working 1 dc in ea st along the top and bottom, and 2 dc in the end of ea row along the sides. Work 3 dc in the corners.

Weave in ends.

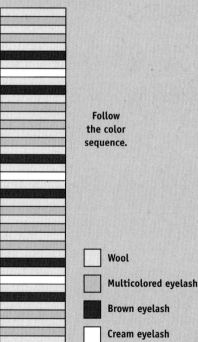

Follow the color sequence.

	Wool
	Multicolored eyelash
	Brown eyelash
	Cream eyelash

felting

Felt in the washer, checking occasionally to see if the blanket is completely felted. When it is felted to the desired texture, adjust to the finished shape and let dry in a warm, dry place.

This project, like the Stiff Yarn Bowl (page 74) was worked in tight stitches with thick roving yarn. The last several rows were repeated without increases so they curled in a little. This ensures that the finished felted project will end up flat, rather than fanning at the edges. I first made this design as a doily in crochet cotton, which is an option for this design.

circular rug

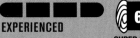

EXPERIENCED

6 SUPER BULKY

Finished Size Before Felting
22" diameter

Finished Size After Felting
18" diameter

Stitches Used
ch
sc
dc
sl st

Gauge in Double Crochet
12 sts and 4 rows = 4"

Note
When counting sts in ea row, ch-2 and ch-3 count as a st.

materials
- 3 balls (78yd/71m) bulky weight novelty yarn*
- Size J (6 mm) hook

*Used in this project: 3 balls Patons' Up Country (100% wool, 78yd/71m, 3.5oz/100g), color #80912, Camel.

felting
Note: Felt only after you have completed all of the crochet instructions at right.

Felt in the washer, checking occasionally to see if the rug is completely felted. When the rug is felted to the desired texture, adjust to the finished shape and let dry in a warm, dry place.

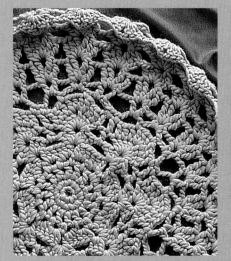

Project before felting.

Project after felting.

instructions

Foundation: Ch 2, turn.

Row 1: 7 sc in 2nd ch from hk, sl st in top of ch-2, pm, do not turn.

Row 2: Ch 1, 2 sc in ea st around, sl st in ch-1 - 16 sts.

Row 3: Ch 4, dc in next st (ch 1, dc in next st) rep around, ch 1 sl st in 3rd ch of ch-4 - 16 ch sps.

Row 4: Sc in ch sp (ch 3, sc in next ch sp) rep around, making last sc in same ch sp as 1st sc - 16 lps.

Row 5: Sl st in next st, sl st in ch sp, ch 3, 2 dc in same ch sp (ch 1, 3 dc in next ch sp) rep around, ch 1, sl st in top of ch-3.

Row 6: Ch 5, (sk 1 ch sp, (3 dc, ch 2, 3 dc) in next ch sp, ch 2) rep 8 times, except on last rep omit last dc and ch 2, then sl st in 3rd ch of ch-5.

Row 7: Sl st in top of next sts until you get to next ch sp between 2 3-dc CLs, sl st in ch sp, ch 3 (3 dc, ch 2, 4 dc) in same ch sp, (ch 1, dc in next ch sp, ch 1, (4 dc, ch 2, 4 dc) in the next ch sp) rep 7 times, ch 1, dc in next ch sp, ch 1, sl st in top of ch-3.

Row 8: Ch 4, dc in next st, ch 1, dc in next st, (ch 1, dc in ch sp) rep 3 times in same ch sp, sk 1 dc, (ch 1, dc in next dc) rep 3 times, [ch 1, dc in next dc, (ch 1, dc in next dc) rep 3 times, (ch 1, dc in ch sp) rep 3 times in same ch sp, sk 1 dc, (ch 1, dc in next st) rep 3 times] rep 7 times, ch 1, dc in next dc, ch 1, sl st in 3rd ch of ch-4.

Row 9: (Ch 5, sk 2 ch sp in 1st rep, sk 3 ch sp in every foll rep, sc in next ch sp, ch 5, sk 2 ch sp, sc in next ch sp, ch 5, sk next 3 ch sp, sc in next ch sp, ch 1, sc in next ch sp) rep 8 times.

Row 10: Sl st in next 3 sts, ch 5, dc in same ch sp, (ch 2, sc in next ch sp, ch 2, sc in same ch sp, ch 2, dc in next ch sp, ch 2 dc in same ch sp, sk next ch sp, ch 2, dc in next ch sp, ch 2 dc in same ch sp) rep around, except on last rep omit last 2 dc and sl st in 3rd ch of ch-5.

Row 11: Ch 3, dc in same ch sp, ch 2, 2 dc in same ch sp, (sk 1 ch sp, ch 2, (2 dc, ch 2, 2 dc) in next ch sp) rep 23 times, ch 2, sl st in top of ch-3.

Row 12 - 15: Sl st to next ch sp, ch 3, 2 dc in same ch sp, ch 2, 3 dc in same ch sp, (sk 1 ch sp, ch 2, (3 dc, ch 2, 3 dc) in next ch sp) rep around, ch 2, sl st in top of ch-3.

Weave in ends.

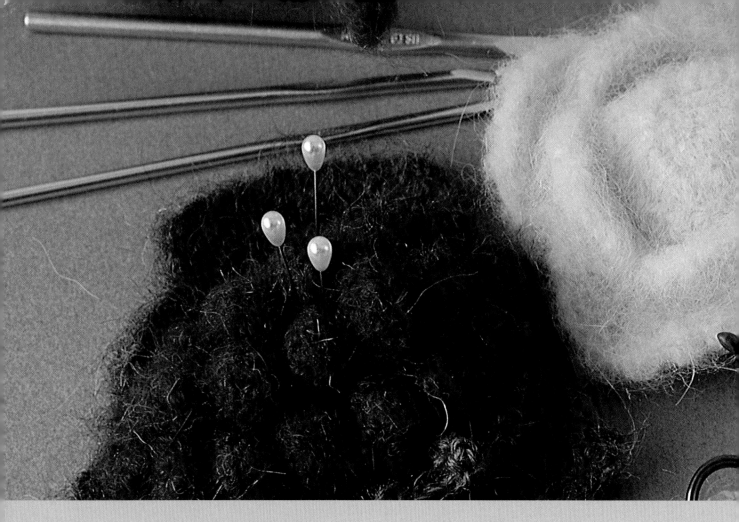

chapter five

for the sewing room

Here are some fun projects to liven up your sewing table. They also make great gifts for any needleworker, from a quilter to a crocheter or a beader. All of the projects can be worked up in a day and then placed in the washer for a fast finish.

Here is an example of using felting for the solid part of the project and then adding decorative crochetwork after the felting is completed. This case protects your favorite scissors at the point and has a nice lacy pattern at the opening.

scissors case

INTERMEDIATE **2 FINE**

Finished Size Before Felting
3" long

Finished Size After Felting
3" long including crochet edging

Stitches Used
ch
hdc
sl st

Gauge in Half Double Crochet (using larger hk)
20 sts and 16 rows = 4"

Project before felting.

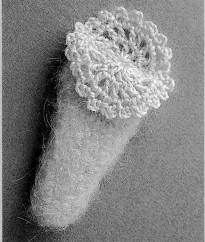

Project after felting.

materials

- 1 ball (126yd/115m) fine weight wool yarn*
- Size F (3.75 mm) hook
- Size C (2.75 mm) hook
- Tapestry needle
- Cotton cord

*Used in this project: 1 ball Dale of Norway's Tiur (100% pure new wool, 126yd/115m, 1.75oz/50g), color #0020 Off-White.

instructions

Foundation: Using the larger hk, ch 3, turn.

Row 1: 8 hdc in 3rd ch from hk, sl st in top of ch-3 to join into a circle, do not turn.

Row 2: Ch 2, (hdc in next 3 sts, 2 hdc in next st) twice, sl st in top of ch-2.

Row 3: Ch 2, (hdc in next 4 sts, 2 hdc in next st) twice, sl st in top of ch-2.

Row 4 and all even rows: Ch 2, hdc in ea st around, sl st in top of ch-2.

Row 5: Ch 2, (hdc in next 5 sts, 2 hdc in next st) twice, sl st in top of ch-2.

Cont inc 2 sts every other row until you work a rep of (hdc in next 8 sts, 2 hdc in next st) twice, work on row even.

Weave in ends.

felting

Baste the opening of the case closed with cotton cord. Felt in the washer, checking occasionally to see if the case is completely felted. When the case is felted to the desired texture, remove the basting cord, adjust to the finished shape and let dry in a warm, dry place.

finishing

Foundation: Using smaller hk and working along outside of felted case opening, sc 20 sts through top edge of felt, sl st in beg st, turn.

Rnd 1: (Ch 1, sk 4, (ch 1, dc) 5 times in same st, ch 2, sk 4, (sl st, ch 3, sl st) in next st) twice.

Rnd 2: [Ch 2, dc in ch sp after 1 dc of shell, ch 2, dc in next dc, (ch 2, dc in next ch sp, ch 2, dc in next dc) twice, ch 2, dc in next ch sp, ch 2, sl st in 1st sl st in corner, ch 2, sc in ch-3 lp, ch 2, sl st in 2nd sl st in corner] twice.

Rnd 3: (Ch 4, sl st in ch sp) rep around.

Weave in ends.

This tool caddy shows how structured felting can be and how you can plan for the funny way felting has of flaring out the edges of openings in projects. The coins in the bottom of the piece act as a weight to offset the tools you will fill the caddy with when it's finished.

tabletop tool caddy

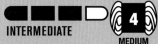
Finished Size Before Felting
4" x 7½"

Finished Size After Felting
3" x 6"

Stitches Used
ch
hdc
sl st

Gauge in Half Double Crochet
13 sts and 10 rows = 4"

Note
Ch-3 and ch-2 count as a st.

Project before felting and assembly.

materials

- 1 ball (60.5yd/55m) bulky weight yarn*
- Size J (6 mm) hook
- About 20 coins or other items to use as weights
- Cotton cord
- Tapestry needle
- Sewing needle and thread to match yarn color

*Used in this project: 1 ball Brown Sheep's Nature's Spectrum (100% wool, 81yd/74m, 2oz/57g) color #W8600 Iris Garden and 1 ball Waverly Wool (100% persian wool, 164yd/151m, 4oz/112g) color #7121 Dark Blue.

instructions

center scissors holder

Foundation: Using solid color yarn, ch 12, turn.

Row 1: Ch 2, hdc in 3rd ch from hk and ea ch across - 13 sts.

Row 2 - 17: Ch 2, hdc in ea st across.

Cut working yarn to 24" from crocheting, pull through last lp on hk and weave in beg tail. Set aside.

variegated crochet hook holders

Foundation: Using multicolored yarn, ch 42, turn.

Row 1: Ch 2, hdc in 3rd ch from hk and ea ch across - 43 sts.

Row 2 - 14: Ch 2, hdc in ea st across.

Weave in ends. Set aside.

circular base pieces

(Make two.)

Foundation: Using solid color yarn, ch 3, turn.

Row 1: 11 hdc in 3rd ch from hk, join to top of ch-3 to form circle.

Row 2: Ch 2, hdc in 1st st, 2 hdc in ea st around, join to top of ch-2 with sl st - 24 sts.

Row 3: Ch 2, hdc in 1st st, (hdc in next st, 2 hdc in next st) rep to last st, hdc in last st, join to top of ch-2 with sl st - 36 sts.

Weave in ends. Set aside.

tabletop tool caddy

assembly

Using the tail from the center scissors holder piece, first stitch the variegated rectangle in place as shown at right, forming each section of the variegated piece into a hump before sewing it in place, so that it will create a little pocket for tools (1). Then, curve the scissors holder piece into a tube and sew the edges together (2). Next, sew one of the round pieces to the bottom of the caddy (3), then baste the last round piece to the first round piece with cotton cord (4).

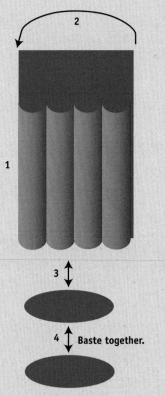

Stitch the pieces together as shown.

felting

Felt in the washer, checking occasionally to see if the caddy is completely felted. When the caddy is felted to the desired texture, remove the basting stitches, adjust to the finished shape and let dry in a warm, dry place.

finishing

Using the sewing needle and thread, sew the bottom circular bases together, inserting the coins before closing completely.

Fun, decorative pincushions are everywhere, and this little bunch of grapes is the perfect gift for a wine lover who also likes needlework. The surface of the grapes is covering the stuffed purple pincushion, so you don't have to make the whole bunch, just the top covering!

grapes pincushion

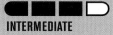

INTERMEDIATE

2 FINE

Finished Size Before Felting
5½"-long

Finished Size After Felting
4½"-long

Stitches Used
ch
sl st
sc
hdc
dc

Gauge in Half Double Crochet
20 sts and 16 rows = 4"

Note
When counting sts in ea row, ch-2 and ch-3 count as a st.

materials

- 2 balls (109yd/100m) sport weight alpaca yarn*:
  - 1 wine
  - 1 green
- Size F (3.75 mm) hook
- Tapestry needle
- Polyester fiberfil

*Used in this project: 2 balls Classic Elite Yarn's Inca Alpaca (100% alpaca, 109yd/100m, 1.75oz/50g), one each in colors #1142 Wine and #1135 Green.

Project before assembly and felting.

instructions
grape leaf

Foundation: Using green yarn, ch 25, turn.

Row 1: Ch 1, sc in the back half of 2nd ch from hk and back half of ea ch to last ch, 5 sc in last ch, sc in other half of rem ch, turn.

Row 2: Ch 1, sk 2, sc in next 23 sts, 2 sc in next 3 sts, sc in next 21 sts, turn.

Row 3: Ch 1, sk 2, sc in next 21 sts, 2 sc in next 3 sts, sc in next 19 sts, turn.

Row 4: Ch 1, sk 2, sc in next 20 sts, 2 sc in next 3 sts, sc in next 21 sts, turn.

Row 5: Ch 1, sk 2, sc in next 20 sts, (2 sc in next st, sc in next st) rep 3 times, sc in next 18 sts, turn.

Row 6: Ch 3, dc in next 21 sts, turn.

Row 7: Ch 3, dc in next 21 sts, turn.

Row 8: Ch 1, sk 1, sc in next 20 sts, turn.

Row 9: Ch 3, dc in next 15 sts, turn.

Row 10: Ch 3, dc in next 15 sts.

Weave in end.

Add a new length of yarn to the base of other side of the leaf and rep rows 6 - 10.

Weave in ends.

grape cluster base

Foundation: Using plum yarn, ch 4, turn.

Row 1: 4 dc in 4th ch from hk, turn - 4 sts.

Row 2: Ch 3, dc in next 4 sts, dc in top of ch-3, turn - 5 sts.

Row 3: Ch 3, dc in next 5 sts, dc in top of ch-3, turn - 6 sts.

Row 4: Ch 3, dc in next 6 sts, dc in top of ch-3, turn - 7 sts.

Row 5: Ch 3, dc in next 7 sts, dc in top of ch-3, turn - 8 sts.

Row 6: Ch 3, dc in next 8 sts, dc in top of ch-3, turn - 9 sts.

Row 7: Ch 3, dc in next 9 sts, dc in top of ch-3, turn - 10 sts.

Work 2 rows even.

Fold last row in half and seam tog.

Weave in ends.

grapes pincushion

grapes

(Make 20 to 25.)

Foundation: Using plum yarn, ch 5, turn.

Row 1: Ch 2, hdc in 3rd ch from hk and next 4 sts, turn - 5 sts.

Row 2 and 3: Ch 2, hdc in ea st, turn.

To gather ends, put the hk through the other 3 corners and make sl st.

Cut yarn to 4" and pull through rem lp.

Set aside.

stem and curling tail

Foundation: Using green yarn, ch 70, turn.

Row 1: (Sk 1, sl st in next st) rep 30 times, sc in next 7 sts, hdc in next 3 sts.

Weave in ends.

assembly

Center the grape cluster base on the leaf and sew in place, stuffing with fiberfil before closing completely. Using the tails of the grapes, sew them in place on the cluster base.

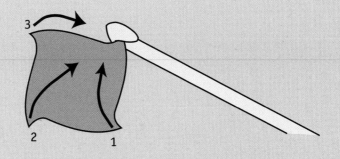

Gather the corners of the grapes as shown.

felting

Felt in the washer, checking occasionally to see if the piece is completely felted. When it is felted to the desired texture, adjust to the finished shape and let dry in a warm, dry place.

finishing

Sew stem and curling vine to leaf.

Here is an alternative to the cut-and-sew flowers on page 66. This flower is made in crochet, stuffed and then felted all at once in the washer, rather than cut and sewn after felting. Either way you make them, you can create a nice decorative item for your sewing table.

flower pincushion

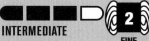

INTERMEDIATE

2 FINE

Finished Size Before Felting
5" diameter

Finished Size After Felting
4½" diameter

Stitches Used
ch
sl st
sc
hdc
dc

Gauge in Half Double Crochet
20 sts and 16 rows = 4"

Note
When counting sts in ea row, ch-2 and ch-3 count as a st.

materials

- 3 balls (109yd/100m) sport weight alpaca yarn*:
  - 1 off-white,
  - 1 yellow green
  - 1 green
- Size F (3.75 mm) hook
- Tapestry needle
- Polyester fiberfil

*Used in this project: 3 balls Classic Elite Yarn's Inca Alpaca (100% alpaca, 109yd/100m, 1.75oz/50g), one each in colors #1116 Cream, #1197 Yellow Green, and #1135 Green.

Project before felting and assembly.

Project after felting.

instructions
small flower section

Foundation: Using off-white yarn, ch 4, turn.

Row 1: 11 dc in 4th ch from hk, sl st in top of ch-4, do not turn.

Row 2: Ch 3, 2 dc in ea st, dc in base of ch-3, sl st in top of ch-3 - 24 sts.

Row 3: Ch 3 (dc in next st, 2 dc in next st) rep 11 times, dc in next st, dc in base of ch-3, sl st in top of ch-3 - 36 sts.

Row 4: (Sk 2, 8 dc in next st, sk 2, sl st in next 4 sts) rep 3 times, sk 2, 8 dc in next st, sk 2, sl st in next 3 sts.

Row 5: (2 dc in 8 sts of next shell, sl st between shells) rep 4 times.

Weave in ends.

large flower section

Beg same as the Small Flower Section above through row 5.

Row 6: 2 dc in ea st on CL, sl st between CLs.

Weave in ends.

leaves

(Make two light green and one green.)

Foundation: Ch 20, turn.

Row 1: Ch 1, working in the back half of the st, 6 sc, 3 hdc, 10 dc, 8 dc in last st, working up other side of sts, 10 dc, 3 hdc, 3 sc, 2 sl st.

Weave in ends.

assembly

Sew the small and large flower sections together along row 4, stuffing with fiberfil before closing completely. Sew leaves to bottom of large flower so they are about halfway beyond the flower. (Use the photos of the finished project as a guide).

felting

Felt in the washer, checking occasionally to see if the pincushion is completely felted. When it is felted to the desired texture, adjust to the finished shape and let dry in a warm, dry place.

This fall-themed pincushion can double as a living room decoration if you choose. Make it really big and it can adorn your hearth through Thanksgiving. The leaf is fun, easy to make and can be gathered or left flat for a variety of arrangements.

pumpkin pincushion

INTERMEDIATE

4 MEDIUM

Finished Size Before Felting
5¼" x 2¼", not including leaf and stem

Finished Size After Felting
4½" x 2"

Stitches Used
ch
hdc
sc

Gauge in Single Crochet
12 sts and 12 rows = 4"

Project before felting and assembly.

materials

- 3 balls (190yd/173m) worsted weight wool yarn*
  - 1 orange
  - 1 green
  - 1 brown
- Size I (5.5 mm) hook
- Stitch marker
- Polyester fiberfil
- Tapestry needle

*Used in this project: 3 balls Brown Sheep's Lamb's Pride (85% wool, 15% mohair, 190yd/173m, 4oz/113g), one each in colors #M97 Rust, #M113 Oregano, and #M89 Roasted Coffee.

instructions
pumpkin

Foundation: Using orange yarn, ch 2, turn.

Rnd 1: 6 sc in 2nd ch from hk, pm, do not turn.

Rnd 2: 2 sc in ea st - 12 sts.

Rnd 3: (Sc in next st, 2 sc in next st) rep 6 times - 18 sts.

Rnd 4: (Sc in next 2 sts, 2 sc in next st) rep 6 times - 24 sts.

Cont with 6 inc in ea rnd until you work a rep of (sc in the next 9 sts, 2 sc in the next st) for a total of 66 sts.

Work even with no inc for 6 rnds.

On next rnd, work a rep of (sc in next 9 sts, sk 1 st, sc in next st) 6 times - 60 sts.

Cont dec 6 sts ea rnd until pumpkin opening is about 2" across.

Stuff the pumpkin with fiberfill and cont in dec patt until opening is almost closed.

Cut the yarn to 24" and weave opening closed. Do not weave in end. It will be used to make pumpkin shape and to sew leaf in place.

leaf

Foundation: Using green yarn, ch 14, turn.

Row 1: Ch 1, sc in 1st half of 2nd ch from hk and 1st half of ea ch to last ch (13 sts total), 5 sc in last ch, working in back half of chs, sc in next 10 ch, turn.

Row 2: Ch 1, sk 1st st, sc in next 10 sts, 2 sc in next 3 sts, sc in next 10 sts, turn.

Row 3: Ch 1, sk 1st st, sc in next 11 sts, 2 sc in next 3 sts, sc in next 9 sts, turn.

Row 4: Ch 1, sk 1st st, sc in next 10 sts, 2 sc in next 3 sts, sc in next 10 sts, turn.

Row 5: Ch 1, sc 1st st, sc in next 23 sts, turn.

Row 6: Ch 3, dc in next 6 sts, hdc in next 2 sts, sc in next 6 sts, hdc in next 2 sts, dc in next 6 sts, turn.

Weave in end.

stem

Foundation: Using brown yarn, ch 2, turn.

Rnd 1: 3 sc in 2nd ch from hk, do not turn.

Rnd 2 - 7: Sc in ea st around.

Cut yarn to 12", do not weave in end.

pumpkin pincushion

assembly

Thread the 24" tail of pumpkin with a tapestry needle and pass through the center of the pumpkin (1). Wrap the yarn around the side of the pumpkin so that it is covering an area of increase stitches. Pass the needle back down through the center of the pumpkin again (2), pulling tightly so that the pumpkin pulls in. Repeat the stitch, creating all six pumpkin sections. Sew the leaf to the top of the pumpkin, then weave in the end on the bottom of the pumpkin. Thread the tail of the stem and sew that to the top of the pumpkin.

felting

Felt in the washer, checking occasionally to see if the pincushion is completely felted. When it is felted to the desired texture, adjust to the finished shape and let dry in a warm, dry place.

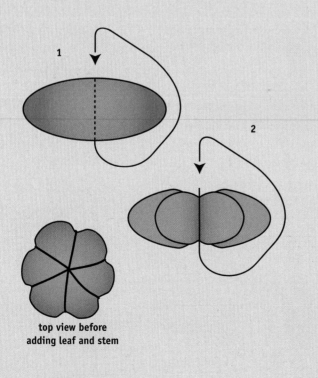

top view before
adding leaf and stem

chapter six

toys

Toys are fun for children and adults alike. It's always special to receive a gift that was made by a loved one, even in today's world of computer and video games. Soft balls are great toys for inside games, and the animals can be a desktop mascot for your favorite grown-up child. You can make the dress pattern for the doll, or make something different to suit your style. Felting the projects when they are already together and stuffed is a quick finish and a fun transformation to watch.

A basic toy for any girl or boy, this simple ball is a great indoor plaything since it's so soft. If you personalize it by embroidering the name of the receiver or a special message, it can become a very cherished possession indeed.

ball

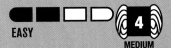

Project before felting.

Project after felting.

Finished Size Before Felting
3½" diameter

Finished Size After Felting
2½"" to 3" diameter

Stitches Used
ch
dc
sl st

Gauge in Double Crochet
8 sts and 14 rows = 4"

Note
When counting sts in ea row, ch-3 and ch-4 count as a st.

To dec 1 dc (dec 1): Yo, hk through next st, yo, pull through st, yo, pull through 2 lps on hk, yo, hk through next st, yo, pull through st, (yo pull through 2 lps) rep 3 times.

materials
- 2 balls (190yd/173m) worsted weight wool yarn*:
  - 1 orange
  - 1 red
- Size H (5 mm) hook
- Polyester fiberfil

*Used in this project: 2 balls Brown Sheep's Lamb's Pride (85% wool, 15% mohair, 190yd/173m, 4oz/113g), one each in colors #M97 Rust and #M81 Red Baron.

instructions

Foundation: Using orange yarn, ch 4, turn.

Row 1: 11 dc in 4th ch from hk, sl st in top of ch-4, do not turn - 12 sts.

Row 2: Ch 3, 2 dc in ea st, dc in base of ch-3, join to top of ch-3 - 24 sts.

Row 3: Ch 3, (dc in next st, 2 dc in next st) rep 11 times, dc in next st, dc in base of ch-3, sl st in top of ch-3 - 30 sts.

Row 4: Change to red yarn, ch 3, dc in ea st, join to top of ch-3.

Row 5: Change to orange yarn, ch 3, dc in ea st, join to top of ch-3.

Row 6: Change to red yarn, ch 3 (dc in next st, dec 1) 9 times, dec 1, join to top of ch-3 - 20 sts.

Stuff ball with fiberfil.

Row 7: Ch 3, dec 1 9 times, join to top of ch 3 - 10 sts.

Weave in ends.

felting

Felt in the washer, checking occasionally to see if the ball is completely felted. When the ball is felted to the desired texture, adjust to the finished shape and let dry in a warm, dry place.

This furry little guy shows how fun and easy it is to whip something up with a little eyelash novelty yarn and feltable wool — in this case, mohair. Add eyes and a nose ... and voilà! You have a friend for life.

hedgehog

EASY · MEDIUM **4** · BULKY **5**

Finished Size Before Felting
4" x 8"

Finished Size After Felting
4" x 7"

Stitches Used
ch
sc

Gauge in Single Crochet
12 sts and 12 rows = 4"

Project before felting.

Project after felting.

materials

- 1 ball (89yd/82m) worsted weight mohair yarn*
- 1 ball (70yd/60m) bulky weight eyelash novelty yarn*
- Size J (6 mm) hook
- Stitch marker
- Fiberfil
- 2 black ³⁄₈" eye buttons
- Black sewing thread and needle
- Size 5 pearl cotton
- Embroidery needle
- Tapestry needle

*Used in this project: 1 ball Ironstone Yarns' English Mohair (78% mohair, 13% wool, 9% nylon, 89yd/82m, 1.4oz/40g), color #923 and 1 ball of Berroco's Zoom (100% polyester, 70yd/60m, 1.75oz/50g), color #9139, Brunette.

instructions

Foundation: Using mohair yarn, ch 2, turn.

Rnd 1: 6 sc in 2nd ch from hk, pm, do not turn.

Rnd 2 - 3: Sc in ea st around.

Rnd 4: 2 sc in ea st around - 12 sts.

Rnd 5 - 7: Sc in ea st around.

Rnd 8: (Sc in next st, 2 sc in next st) rep 6 times - 18 sts.

Rnd 9: Sc in ea st around.

Rnd 10: Holding eyelash and mohair tog as 1, sc in ea st around.

Rnd 11: (Sc in next 2 sts, 2 sc in next st) rep 6 times - 24 sts.

Rnd 12 - 14: Sc in ea st around.

Rnd 15: (Sc in next 3 sts, 2 sc in next st) rep 6 times - 30 sts.

Rnd 16 - 18: Sc in ea st around.

Rnd 19: (Sc in next 4 sts, 2 sc in next st) rep 6 times - 36 sts.

Rnd 20 - 22: Sc in ea st around.

Rnd 23: (Sc in next 5 sts, 2 sc in next st) rep 6 times - 42 sts.

Rnd 24 - 26: Sc in ea st around.

Rnd 27: (Sc in next 5 sts, sk next st, sc in next st) rep 6 times - 36 sts.

Rnd 28: (Sc in next 4 sts, sk next st, sc in next st) rep 6 times - 30 sts.

Rnd 29: (Sc in next 3 sts, sk next st, sc in next st) rep 6 times - 24 sts.

Stuff hedgehog with fiberfil.

Rnd 30: (Sc in next 2 sts, sk next st, sc in next st) rep 6 times - 18 sts.

Rnd 31: (Sc in next st, sk next st, sc in next st) rep 6 times - 12 sts.

Rnd 32: (Sk next st, sc in next st) rep 6 times - 6 sts.

Weave in ends.

felting

Felt in the washer, checking occasionally to see if hedgehog is completely felted. When the animal is felted to the desired texture, adjust to the finished shape and let dry in a warm, dry place.

finishing

Sew button eyes to head with the needle and thread. Embroider the nose with pearl cotton and the embroidery needle. Trim mohair on face.

Balls and tubes transform into a cute little teddy bear, small enough to fit in a purse and easy enough to make in a weekend.

teddy bear

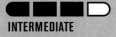
INTERMEDIATE

4 MEDIUM

Finished Size Before Felting
5½" tall

Finished Size After Felting
4½" tall

Stitches Used
ch

sc

sl st

Gauge in Single Crochet
14 sts and 12 rows = 4"

Note
When counting sts in ea row, ch-2 and ch-3 count as a st.

materials

- 1 ball (218yd/200m) worsted weight wool yarn*
- Size H (5 mm) hook
- Stitch marker
- 2 ¼" spacer beads
- 2 size 11 seed beads
- Sewing needle and thread to match beads
- Black 6-strand embroidery floss
- Embroidery needle

Optional: 12" ribbon (½"-wide)

*Used in this project: 1 ball Knit One Crochet Too's Parfait Solids (100% pure wool, 218yd/200m, 3.5oz/100g), color #1893.

instructions

body

Foundation: Ch 2, turn.

Rnd 1: 6 sc in 2nd ch from hk, pm, do not turn.

Rnd 2: 2 sc in ea st - 12 sts.

Rnd 3: (Sc in next st, 2 sc in next st) rep 6 times - 18 sts.

Rnd 4: (Sc in next 2 sts, 2 sc in next st) rep 6 times - 24 sts.

Rnd 5: (Sc in next 3 sts, 2 sc in next st) rep 6 times - 30 sts.

Rnd 6: (Sc in next 4 sts, 2 sc in next st) rep 6 times - 36 sts.

Rnd 7 - 14: Work even in sc.

(Dec section)

Rnd 15: (Sc in next 4 sts, sk 1, sc in next st) rep 6 times - 30 sts.

Rnd 16: (Sc in next 3 sts, sk 1, sc in next st) rep 6 times - 24 sts.

Rnd 17: (Sc in next 2 sts, sk 1, sc in next st) rep 6 times - 18 sts.

Stuff body with fiberfil.

Rnd 18: (Sc in next st, sk 1, sc in next st) rep 6 times - 12 sts.

Rnd 19: (Sk 1, sc in next st) rep 6 times - 6 sts.

Weave in ends.

head

Foundation: Ch 2, turn.

Rnd 1: 6 sc in 2nd ch from hk, pm, do not turn.

Rnd 2: (Sc in next 2 sts, 2 sc in next st) twice - 8 sts.

Rnd 3: (Sc in next 3 sts, 2 sc in next st) twice - 10 sts.

Rnd 4: (Sc in next st, 2 sc in next st) rep 5 times - 15 sts.

Rnd 5: (Sc in next 2 sts, 2 sc in next st) rep 5 times - 20 sts.

Rnd 6: (Sc in next 3 sts, 2 sc in next st) rep 5 times - 25 sts.

Rnd 7 - 11: Work even in sc.

Rnd 12: (Sc in next 3 sts, sk 1, sc in next st) rep 5 times - 20 sts.

Stuff head with fiberfil.

Rnd 13: (Sc in next 2 sts, sk 1, sc in next st) rep 5 times - 15 sts.

Rnd 14: (Sc in next st, sk 1, sc in next st) rep 5 times - 10 sts.

Rnd 15: (Sk 1, sc in next st) rep 5 times - 5 sts.

Weave in ends.

teddy bear

legs

(Make two.)

Foundation: Ch 4, turn.

Rnd 1: 11 dc in 4th ch from hk, sl st in top of ch-4, pm, do not turn.

Rnd 2: Sc in ea st around, sc in sl st - 12 sts.

Rnd 3 - 5: Sc in ea st.

Rnd 6: (Sc in next 2 sts, sk 1, sc in next st) rep 3 times - 9 sts.

Rnd 7: (Sc in next st, sk 1, sc in next st) rep 3 times - 6 sts.

Cut yarn to 12" and pull through last lp.

Stuff leg with fiberfil.

Set aside.

arms

(Make two.)

Foundation: Ch 2, turn.

Rnd 1: 9 sc in 2nd ch from hk, pm, do not turn.

Rnd 2 - 10: Sc in ea st.

Cut yarn to 12" and pull through last lp.

Stuff arms with fiberfill.

Set aside.

assembly

Sew head to top of body. Using the 12" tails of yarn, sew the legs and arms to the body.

ears

Attach a new length of yarn to 10th rnd right side of the head where you want the ear to begin.

Sk 1 st, 7 dc in next st, sk 1 st, sl st in next st.

Weave in ends.

Rep for the other ear, beg next ear on the same row of the head 3 sts away from the ending of 1st ear.

tail

Foundation: Ch 3, turn.

Row 1: Ch 1, sc in 2nd ch from hk and next 2 ch.

Cut yarn to 6" and pull through last lp. Sew to back of body.

felting

Felt by hand until matted, then either continue felting by hand or felt in the washer, checking occasionally until the yarn is completely felted. Adjust to the desired shape and let dry in a warm, dry place.

finishing

Sew the bead eyes to the face by stringing one large bead and one small bead, then passing back through the large bead.

Use the embroidery floss to sew the nose in satin stitch and the mouth with backstitches.

Tie the ribbon around the neck and make the ends into a bow.

Wool and sheep go together, so how could we not have a sheep in this book? Although the fluffy part isn't the wool that felts, this fluffy black-and-white sheep is a cute addition to a yarn basket that adds a little character to the mix.

little white lamb

Finished Size Before Felting
  5" x 7½", including legs
and head

Finished Size After Felting
  4" x 6½", including legs
and head

Stitches Used
  ch
  sc
  dc
  sl st

Gauge in Single Crochet
(using small hk and wool yarn)
  16 sts and 18 rows = 4"

materials

- 1 ball (223yd/204m) black
  worsted weight wool yarn*
- 1 ball (223yd/204m) off-white
  worsted weight wool yarn*
- 1 ball (47yd/43m) white
  bulky weight novelty yarn*
- Size I (6.5 mm) hook
- Size N (10 mm) hook
- Stitch marker
- Polyester fiberfil

*Used in this project: 1 ball each
Patons' Classic Wool (100% pure new
wool, 223yd/204m, 3.5oz/100g),
colors #226 Black and #202 Aran
and Allure (100% nylon, 47yd/43m,
1.75oz/50g), color #4005 Diamond.

Project before felting.

instructions
body

Foundation: Using white novelty yarn and off-white wool held tog as 1 and working with the larger hk, ch 4, turn.

Row 1: 9 dc in 4th ch from hk, sl st in top of ch-4, do not turn.

Row 2: Ch 3, 2 dc in ea st around, dc in base of ch-3, sl st in top of ch-3 - 20 sts.

Weave in ends.

Rep to make another piece, but do not cut yarn or weave in end.

Place pieces tog and working through both edges, sc in ea st along edge, seaming pieces tog and stuffing with fiberfil before closing seam with last sts.

Cut the working yarn to about 12" and pull through last lp. Use 12" tail to sew head to body.

head

Foundation: Using black yarn and smaller hk, ch 2, turn.

Rnd 1: 6 sc in 2nd ch from hk, pm, do not turn.

Rnd 2: Sc in ea st.

Rnd 3: 2 sc in ea st - 12 sts.

Rnd 4 - 7: Work even in sc.

Rnd 8: Change to novelty yarn and off-white wool held tog as 1, and work even, pulling sts out about ½" so you can use the larger hk for the next rnd.

Rnd 9 -11: Change to larger hk and work even.

Rnd 12: (1 sc, sk 1 st, 1 sc) 4 times - 8 sts.

Stuff head with fiberfil.

Rnd 13: (Sk 1 st, 1 sc) 4 times - 4 sts.

Weave in ends.

legs

(Make four.)

Foundation: Using black yarn and smaller hk, ch 2, turn.

Rnd 1: 5 sc in 2nd ch from hk, pm, do not turn.

Rnd 2 - 7: Sc in ea st around.

Cut yarn to 6" and pull through last lp, set aside

little white lamb

ears

(Make two.)

Foundation: Using black yarn and smaller hk, ch 7, turn.

Row 1: Ch 1, sc in 2nd ch from hk and ea ch across, turn - 7 sts.

Row 2: Ch 1, sc in next 4 sts, sl st in next 3 sts.

Cut yarn to 6" and pull through last lp, set aside.

tail

Using novelty yarn and off-white wool yarn held tog as 1 with the larger hk, ch 5, cut yarn to 6" and pull through last lp. Set aside.

assembly

Using the tails from the individual pieces threaded with a tapestry needle, sew the parts onto the body, following the general placement as shown in the finished piece.

felting

Felt in the washer, checking occasionally to see if the lamb is completely felted. When the lamb is felted to the desired texture, adjust to the finished shape and let dry in a warm, dry place.

finishing

Sew the bead eyes in place with the needle and thread.

This versatile pattern is easily made into the perfect gift for that special person. Notice how different the two variations shown in the photos on the following pages are just by changing the treatment of the eyes; one has button eyes, while the other has embroidered eyes. Using matching skin-colored yarn, and making the same-colored eyes and favorite-colored dress can make this just the right doll for anyone you choose.

doll

Finished Size Before Felting

14" tall

Finished Size After Felting

Approximately 12" tall

Stitches Used

ch

dc

Gauge in Single Crochet

(using wool yarn and larger hk)

14 sts and 12 rows = 4"

Note

When counting sts in ea row, ch-2 and ch-3 count as a st.

materials

- 1 ball (223yd/204m) worsted weight wool yarn*
- 1 ball (136yd/125m) fine weight cotton yarn*
- 1 ball (47yd/43m) worsted weight novelty yarn*
- Size H (5 mm) hook
- Size F (3.75 mm) hook
- Embroidery thread
  - 1 skein red
  - 1 skein black (optional)
- Embroidery needle
- Tapestry needle
- 2 ½"-wide buttons (optional)
- Stitch marker

*Used in this project: 1 ball each Patons' Classic Wool (100% pure new wool, 223yd/204m, 3.5oz/100g), colors #202 Aran and Patons' Grace (100% mercerized cotton, 136yd/125m, 1.75oz/50g), color #6032 Viola, and Patons' Cha Cha (100% nylon, 77yd/70m, 1.75oz/50g), color # 2018 Soul.

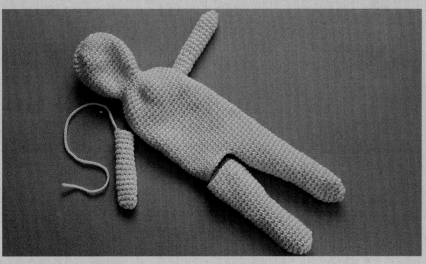

Project before felting.

instructions
doll

(Starting at top of head.)

Foundation: Using wool yarn and larger hk, ch 2, turn.

Rnd 1: 6 sc in 2nd ch from hk, pm, do not turn.

Rnd 2: 2 sc in ea st - 12 sts.

Rnd 3: (Sc in next st, 2 sc in next st) rep 6 times - 18 sts.

Rnd 4: (Sc in next 2 sts, 2 sc in next st) rep 6 times - 24 sts.

Rnd 5: (Sc in next 3 sts, 2 sc in next st) rep 6 times - 30 sts.

Rnd 6 - 15: Work even in sc.

(Decrease for neck section)

Rnd 16: (Sc in next 3 sts, sk 1, sc in next st) rep 6 times - 24 sts.

Rnd 17: (Sc in next 2 sts, sk 1, sc in next st) rep 6 times - 18 sts.

(Neck)

Rnd 18 - 19: Work even in sc.

shoulders

Rnd 20: (Sc in next 2 sts, 2 sc in next st) rep 6 times - 24 sts.

Rnd 21: (Sc in next 3 sts, 2 sc in next st) rep 6 times - 30 sts.

Rnd 22: (Sc in next 4 sts, 2 sc in next st) rep 6 times - 36 sts.

torso

Rnd 23 - 47: Work even in sc.

one leg

Rnd 48: Ch 2, sk 18, sc in next 18 sts - 18 sts and 2 ch.

Rnd 49: Sc in 2 ch, sc in next 18 sts - 20 sts.

Rnd 50 - 54: Work even in sc.

Rnd 55: Dec 1 st at inside leg - 19 sts.

Rnd 56: Work even in sc.

Rnd 57 - 64: Rep rows 55 - 56 - 18, 17, 16, 15 sts.

Rnd 65 - 73: Work even in sc.

Rnd 74: (3 sc, sk 1, sc) rep 3 times - 12 sts.

Rnd 75: (2 sc, sk 1, sc) rep 3 times - 9 sts.

Rnd 76: (Sc, sk 1, sc) rep 3 times - 3 sts.

Weave in ends.

separate leg

Foundation: Using wool yarn and larger hk, ch 20, join into a circle with sl st - 20 sts.

Rnd 1 - 6: work even in sc.

Rnd 7 - 28: Rep rows 55 - 76 from "One leg" section.

doll

arms

(Make two.)

Foundation: Using wool yarn and larger hk, ch 2, turn.

Rnd 1: 6 sc in 2nd ch from hk.

Rnd 2: (Sc, 2 sc in next st) rep 3 times - 9 sts.

Rnd 3 - 15: Work even in sc.

Cut yarn to 10", pull through last st. Thread with tapestry needle and sew to sides of doll near shoulders.

Weave in ends.

felting

Stuff the body, head and leg with fiberfil; stuff the other leg with fiberfil. Sew the leg to the body. Felt by hand until matted, then either continue felting by hand or felt in the washer, checking occasionally until the yarn is completely felted. Adjust to the desired shape and let dry in a warm, dry place.

hair and face

Using the sewing needle and thread, either sew buttons on for eyes or embroider them in black. Then, stitch mouth with red floss, using straight stitches to make the heart shape. Using a tapestry needle and the novelty yarn, sew hair on head with loose backstitches until covering the desired amount. Weave in ends.

dress

The size of the dress needed will depend on how small your doll felts, which can vary greatly. The bodice is also dependent on where you attach the arms. Here are instructions for the dress for the size doll that my project ended.

skirt

Foundation: Using smaller hk and cotton yarn, ch 22, turn.

Row 1: Ch 7, dc in 8th ch from hk, (ch 1, sk 1, dc in next ch) rep 11 times, turn.

Row 2: Ch 3, dc in 1st ch sp, (ch 1, dc in next ch sp) rep 11 times, turn.

Row 3: Ch 7, dc in 1st ch sp, (ch 1, dc in next ch sp) rep 11 times, turn.

Row 4 - 39: Rep row 2 - 3.

Row 40: Rep row 2.

Row 41: To attach the ends into a tube, ch 7, dc in 1st ch sp, dc in 2nd ch sp of other end of skirt, (dc in next ch sp on last row, dc in next ch sp on first row) rep across.

Turn inside-out so seam is on the inside of the skirt.

bodice

Row 1: Working along the end of the tube, ch 3, dc in the end of ea ch-3 or dc across, sl st in the top of the ch-3 - 42 sts.

Row 2 - 3: Ch 3, dc in ea st around, sl st in top of ch-3.

Row 4: (armhole) Ch 3, dc in next 8 sts, cut yarn, weave in end, sk 3 sts, attach new yarn, ch 3, dc in next 19 sts, cut yarn, weave in

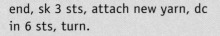

end, sk 3 sts, attach new yarn, dc in 6 sts, turn.

Row 5: Ch 3, dc in next 6 sts, dc in top of ch-3, ch 3, dc in next 19 sts, dc in top of ch-3, ch 3, dc in next 8 sts, turn.

Row 6: Ch 3 dc in ea st across, turn.

Row 7: Ch 3, (sk next st, dc in next 2 sts) rep 14 times.

Weave in ends.

Make 6"-long ch and use as a ribbon to tie the back opening of the dress closed at the neckline.

Always check with your local yarn or craft stores for crocheting supplies, tools, embellishments and books.

supply sources

yarn companies

Baabajoes Wool Company
P.O. Box 260604
Lakewood, CO 80226
www.baabajoeswool.com

Bernat, Patons and Lily Yarns
P.O. Box 40
Listowel, Ontario, Canada N4W 3H3
www.bernat.com
www.patonsyarns.com
www.lilyyarns.com

Berroco, Inc.
P.O. Box 367
14 Elmdale Road
Uxbridge, MA 01569
www.berroco.com

Brown Sheep Co., Inc.
100662 County Road 16
Mitchell, NE 69357
www.brownsheep.com

Blue Sky Alpacas, Inc.
P.O. Box 387
St. Francis, MN 55070
www.blueskyalpacas.com

Cascade Yarns
1224 Andover Park E
Tukwila, WA 98188
(800) 548-1048
www.cascadeyarns.com

Classic Elite Yarns
122 Western Ave.
Lowell, MA 01851
www.classiceliteyarns.com

Crystal Palace Yarns
160 23rd St.
Richmond, CA 94804
(510) 237-9988
www.straw.com

Dale of Norway
N16 W23390 Stoneridge Drive, #A
Waukesha, WI 53188
(262) 544-1996
www.dale.no

Harrisville Designs
P.O. Box 806
Harrisville, NH 03450
(603) 827-3333
www.harrisville.com

Ironstone Yarns
P.O. Box 8
Las Vegas, NM 87701

JCA, Artful Yarns, Reynolds
35 Scales Lane
Townsend, MA 01469-1094

Knit One Crochet Too
91 Tandberg Trail, Unit 6
Windham, ME 04062
www.knitonecrochettoo.com

Knitting Fever, Inc.
35 Debevoise Ave.
Roosevelt, NY 11575
(516) 546-3600
www.knittingfever.com

Lion Brand
34 W. 15th St.
New York, NY 10011
(800) 258-9276
www.lionbrand.com

Mountain Colors
P.O. Box 156
Corvallis, MT 59828
(406) 961-1900
www.mountaincolors.com

Plymouth Yarn
P.O. Box 28
Bristol, PA 19007
(215) 788-0459
www.plymouthyarn.com

Rowan, Jaeger
Westminster Fibers
4 Townsend W Unit 8
Nashua, NH 03063

Tahki-StacyCharles and Filatura Di Crosa
70-30 80th St., Building 36
Ridgewood, NY 11384
(800) 338-yarn
www.tahkistacycharles.com

Trendsetter Yarns
16745 Saticoy St, #101
Van Nuys, CA 91406
www.trendsetteryarns.com

embellishments

Bead Heaven
A division of Halcraft USA, Inc.
New York, NY 10010
www.halcraft.com

Blue Moon Beads
7855 Hayvenhurst Ave.
Van Nuys, CA 91406
www.bluemoonbeads.com

The Caron Collection
55 Old South Ave.
Stratford, CT 06615-7315
www.caron-net.com

Cousin Corporation
P.O. Box 2939
Largo, FL 33779
(800) 366-2687
www.cousin.com

Creative Castle
2321 Michael Drive
Newbury Park, CA 91320-3233
(805) 499-1377
www.creativecastle.com

Darice
13000 Darice Parkway, Park 82
Strongsville, OH 44149
(866) 432-7423
www.darice.com

Fire Mountain Gems and Beads
1 Fire Mountain Way
Grants Pass, OR 97526-2373
(800) 423-2319
www.firemountaingems.com

JHB International
1955 S. Quince St.
Denver, CO 80231
(303) 751-8100
www.buttons.com

LaMode Buttons
Blumenthal Lansing Co.
Lansing, IA 52151
www.buttonsplus.com

Rings & Things
P.O. Box 450
214 N. Wall St., Suite 990
Spokane, WA 99210-0450
(509) 624-8565
www.rings-things.com

crocheting tools

Boye
A product of Wrights
85 South St.
West Warren, MA 01092
www.wrights.com

Brittany Hooks and Needles
(707) 877-1881
www.brittanyneedles.com

Clover Needlecraft, Inc.
13438 Alondra Blvd.
Cerritos, CA 90703
www.clover-usa.com

Crystal Palace Yarns
160 23rd St
Richmond, CA 94804
www.straw.com

Susan Bates
A product of Coats & Clark
P.O. Box 12229
Greenville, SC 29612
(800) 648-1479
www.coatsandclark.com

supply sources

other resources

Annie's Attic
1 Annie Lane
Big Sandy, TX 75755
(800) 582-6643
www.anniesattic.com

Crochet Guild of America (CGOA)
P.O. Box 3388
Zanesville, OH 43702-3388
(740) 452-4541
www.crochet.org

Craft Yarn Council of America (CYCA)
P.O. Box 9
Gastonia, NC 28053
(704) 824-7838
www.craftyarncouncil.com

Home Sew
P.O. Box 4099
Bethlehem, PA 18018-0099
(800) 344-4739
www.homesew.com

KP Books
700 E. State St.
Iola, WI 54990-0001
(888) 457-2873
www.krause.com

Mary Maxim
2001 Holland Ave
P.O. Box 5019
Port Huron, MI 48061-5019
(800) 962-9504
www.marymaxim.com

The National NeedleArts Association (TNNA)
P.O. Box 3388
1100-H Brandywine Blvd.
Zanesville, OH 43702-3388
(740) 455-6773
www.TNNA.org

index

more creative ideas from Jane Davis

Decorative Wirework

Beautifully illustrated with easy-to-follow instructions, readers are guided through the techniques used to create more than 50 projects for jewelry and home decor, such as brooches, bracelets, ornaments, and more.

Softcover • 8¼ x 10⅞
128 pages
100+ color photos, 100+ illus.
Item# DCWK • $19.95

The Complete Guide to Beading Techniques

30 Decorative Projects

This complete volume of beading techniques is filled with gorgeous photos of antique and contemporary beadwork. Features 30 step-by-step projects.

Softcover • 8¼ x 10⅞
160 pages
100 illus. • 150 color photos
Item# BEHME • $24.95

A Beader's Reference

With three pattern sections, a project section with instructions for 12 projects, and a contributing artists' gallery, this indispensable beader's tool provides hundreds of patterns.

Softcover • 8¼ x 10⅞
160 pages
300+ charts & illus.
100 color photos
Item# BDREF • $24.99

Bead Embroidery The Complete Guide

Bring New Dimension to Classic Needlework

This portable and durable resource features 20 projects, complete with 200 color illustrations that use bead embroidery stitches with a variety of materials. The selection of quick and easy embellishments and intensive endeavors include adding fringe to a pillow, creating a zippered notions case, coin purse, Christmas ornament, sachet pillow and more.

Hardcover w/spiral • 5⅝ x 7⅝
256 pages
200+ color photos and illus.
Item# BDEM • $29.99

Knit Ponchos, Wraps & Scarves

Create 40 Quick and Contemporary Accessories

Answering the demand for new scarf, poncho and shawl ideas, this book provides 40 fun, contemporary projects knitters can create quickly and easily, many featuring popular novelty yarns. Includes projects for all skill levels.

Softcover • 8¼ x 10⅞
128 pages
100 color photos, 125 illus.
Item# SCVSH • $21.99